Reclaiming Democracy

Reclaiming Democracy

The Social Justice and Political Economy of Gregory Baum and Kari Polanyi Levitt

EDITED BY

MARGUERITE MENDELL

McGill-Queen's University Press
Montreal & Kingston · London · Ithaca

ISBN 0-7735-2870-9

Legal deposit third quarter 2005
Bibliothèque nationale du Québec

Printed in Canada on acid-free paper that is 100% ancient forest free (100% post-consumer recycled), processed chlorine free.

McGill-Queen's University Press acknowledges the support of the Canada Council for the Arts for our publishing program. We also acknowledge the financial support of the Government of Canada through the Book Publishing Industry Development Program (BPIDP) for our publishing activities.

Library and Archives Canada Cataloguing in Publication

Reclaiming democracy : the social justice and Political Economy of Gregory Baum and Kari Polanyi Levitt / edited by Marguerite Mendell.
Includes bibliographical references.
ISBN 0-7735-2870-9
1. Democracy – Canada. 2. Democracy – Caribbean Area. 3. Canada – Economic conditions. 4. Caribbean Area – Economic conditions. 5. Social justice – Canada. 6. Social justice – Caribbean Area. 7. Economics – Sociological aspects. 8. Social justice. 9. Democracy. I. Mendell, Marguerite, 1947–
HM671.R42 2005 306.3 C2005-900098-8

Typeset in Sabon 10/12
by Caractéra inc., Quebec City

Contents

POLITICAL ECONOMY AND DEMOCRACY

List of Contributors

SAMIR AMIN Director, The Third World Forum, Dakar, Senegal. A leading political economist and a world-renowned Neo-Marxian thinker, he cofounded The World Forum for Alternatives, created in 1997 to service the needs of social movements engaged in the globalization discourse. In his volume, *Obsolescent Capitalism: Contemporary Politics and Global Disorder*, this foremost thinker on the changing dynamic of capitalism discusses how the U.S. economic preponderance is determining the future of capitalistic development.

GREGORY BAUM Professor Emeritus, Theological Ethics and Sociology of Religion, McGill University, Montreal. An officer of the Order of Canada, Professor Baum is editor of *The Ecumenist* and a member of the editorial board of *Rélations*, a francophone Catholic monthly published in Quebec. A leading contemporary theologian and an important contributor to the understanding of religion and spirituality in the context of modern human experiences, he is presently a faculty lecturer in ethics at McGill University.

LLOYD BEST Director, The Trinidad and Tobago Institute of the West Indies, St Augustine, Trinidad. A well-respected thinker in the Caribbean and internationally on social and political issues, he is the founder of the *New World Quarterly* and publisher of *Trinidad and Tobago Review*. He received the Order of the Caribbean Community in July 2002.

DUNCAN CAMERON Associate Professor, Department of Political Science, University of Ottawa, Ottawa. Former president, Canadian Centre for Policy Alternatives, Professor Cameron has written extensively on North American free trade, national and international political economy, and ethics and economics.

URSULA FRANKLIN Professor Emerita, Department of Materials Science Engineering, and Senior Resident and Fellow, Massey College, University of Toronto, Toronto. Professor Franklin, feminist, Quaker, and peace activist, has made an outstanding contribution to our understanding of the human dimensions of science and technology and to peaceful co-existence. She was instrumental in organizing the Voice of Women, one of Canada's first feminist organizations and is an advocate of the international Science for Peace organization. Professor Franklin is a companion of the Order of Canada and fellow of the Royal Society of Canada.

NORMAN GIRVAN Professorial Research Fellow, Institute of International Relations, University of West Indies, St Augustine, Trinidad, and secretary general of the Association of Caribbean States (2001–04). A professor of development studies, he is well known in the Caribbean for his work on Caribbean development and integration.

DENIS GOULET Professor Emeritus of Economics, University of Notre Dame, Indiana. Professor Goulet is a pioneer in the interdisciplinary study of development ethics. He is presently William and Dorothy O'Neal Chair in Education for Justice, Department of Economics, Faculty Fellow, Kellogg Institute for International Studies, and Faculty Fellow, Joan B. Kroc Institute for International Peace Studies, University of Notre Dame, Indiana.

KARI POLANYI LEVITT Professor Emerita of Economics, McGill University, Montreal. Honorary president, Karl Polanyi Institute of Political Economy, Concordia University, Montreal. A founding member of the Canadian Association for the Study of International Development (CASID), Professor Polanyi Levitt has published extensively on international and Caribbean political economy and the work of Karl Polanyi. Her seminal *Silent Surrender* (1970) was reprinted in 2003 with a new introduction.

MARGUERITE MENDELL Vice-principal and Associate Professor, School of Community and Public Affairs, and Director, Karl Polanyi Institute of Political Economy, Concordia University, Montreal.

Professor Mendell has published widely on Karl Polanyi and on alternative democratically based economic development strategies in Quebec and abroad.

ARVIND SHARMA Birks Professor of Comparative Religion at McGill University, Montreal. Professor Sharma is a leading scholar on Hinduism, world religions, and issues concerning women and religion. He advocates the adoption of a Universal Declaration of Human Rights by the world's religions.

CAROLYN SHARP Assistant Professor, Faculty of Theology, Saint Paul's University, Ottawa, and member, Board of Directors, Saint Paul University Ethics Centre. Professor Sharp has written extensively on feminist liberation theologists.

MEL WATKINS Professor Emeritus of Economics and Political Science, University of Toronto. Professor Watkins has published extensively in the area of Canadian political economy. He is a columnist for *This Magazine* and for the on-line review *Straight Goods*. He is past president of Science for Peace (Canada), a Canadian organization concerned with peace, justice, and environmental sustainability.

MICHAEL WITTER Senior Lecturer and Head, Department of Economics, University of the West Indies, Mona Campus, Kingston, Jamaica. Professor Witter has served as consultant for several international organizations, private Jamaican and international companies as well as the governments of Jamaica and Belize.

Acronyms and Abbreviations List

ACE	Association of Caribbean Economists
ACS	Association of Caribbean States
ANC	African National Congress
AUCC	Association of Universities and Colleges of Canada
CARIBCAN	Caribbean/Canada Trade Agreement
CAPMO	Carrefour de pastorale en monde ouvrier
CARICOM	Caribbean Community
CASID	Canadian Association for the Study of International Development
CBI	Caribbean Basin Initiative
CEPAL	Comisión Económica para América Latina y el Caribe
CIDA	Canadian International Development Agency
CPMO	Centre de pastorale en milieu ouvrier
CSME	Caribbean Single Market and Economy
GNP	Gross National Product
HEC	École des Hautes Études Commerciales, Université de Montréal
IDEP	United Nations African Institute for Development and Planning
ISER	Institute of Social and Economic Research, Jamaica
LSE	London School of Economics
MNC	multinational corporation
Mona	Mona Campus of the University of the West Indies
NCPE	New Canadian Political Economy
NDP	New Democratic Party (Canada)
NEP	New Economic Policy

NGO Non-governmental Organization
OECS Organization of Eastern Caribbean States
PC-OSATU (South Africa) Coalition between South African Communist Party and the Congress of South African Trade Unions
PNM Peoples National Movement, Trinidad
PRI Partido Revolucionario Institucional, Mexico
T&T Trinidad and Tobago
TNC transnational corporation
UNIP United National Independence Party, Trinidad
UWI University of the West Indies

Acknowledgments

The conference to celebrate the life and work of Kari Polanyi Levitt and Gregory Baum, hosted by the Karl Polanyi Institute of Political Economy, Concordia University, Montreal, in October 1998, received generous support from several organizations and institutions. I wish to thank the Faculty of Arts and Science, Concordia University, the Centre for Continuing Education, Concordia University, the International Development Research Centre (Ottawa), le Ministère de l'éducation, Gouvernement du Québec, the Samuel and Saidye Bronfman Family Foundation, the Laidlaw Foundation, Rélations, les Sœurs de bon conseil, the Faculty of Religious Studies, McGill University, and the United Theological College for their financial contributions to this event. I am very grateful to Dr Barry Levy, dean, Faculty of Religious Studies, McGill University for his cooperation and involvement in this publication of the conference proceedings.

My special thanks to Duncan Cameron, professor of political science, who chaired the entire conference with his remarkable skill, panache, and humour. Scholar and activist, former editor of the *Canadian Forum*, former president of the Centre for Policy Alternatives, critical political economist, Duncan Cameron's contributions to Canadian political debate are well known. He has also worked closely with both Kari Polanyi Levitt and Gregory Baum over many years and during the conference made the links between their respective work as few others could have done.

Finally, it has become impossible to find words that are adequate to thank Ana Gomez, administrative coordinator of the Polanyi Institute and tireless co-worker. Ana Gomez is synonymous with the Polanyi Institute and its many projects. This project was no exception. She was instrumental to all aspects of this event, from conference organization to the preparation of this manuscript. She is truly a blessing and a delightful friend. My deepest appreciation to Ana for everything she does, for never saying no, for never giving up, and for always smiling.

Reclaiming Democracy

Introduction

MARGUERITE MENDELL

THE BENEFIT OF TIME

In the fall of 1998, the Karl Polanyi Institute of Political Economy invited friends, colleagues, students, and the public to celebrate the seventy-fifth birthdays of two leading Canadian scholars, Kari Polanyi Levitt and Gregory Baum. This was a wonderful occasion. The presence of at least three generations confirmed what we already knew: the influence of these two remarkable people continues to grow as young people discover Kari and Gregory through their teaching, writings, and many public appearances in Canada and abroad. The participation of eminent scholars such as Samir Amin, Ursula Franklin, Mel Watkins, and others testifies to the enduring contribution of these two scholars to intellectual and political discourse. Their reach is broad; like those whose tributes fill the pages of this celebratory volume in their honour, Kari and Gregory are organic intellectuals who have bridged the divide between academic scholarship and popular engagement. Their contribution to critical thought has never been more urgently needed. Kari and Gregory have participated in challenging debates, stimulating and provoking critical thinking and controversy for almost five decades. The authors in this volume celebrate the important place Kari and Gregory occupy as critical scholars and public intellectuals and to their impact on scholarship and activism. They speak to Kari and Gregory's lifelong commitment to social justice. They speak of friendship and generosity.

While the book is divided into two parts, one dedicated to Kari Polanyi Levitt, the other to Gregory Baum, many of the individuals who participated not only know each other but have shared experiences over the years in Quebec, in Canada, and abroad. It is not a coincidence that a single book pays tribute to a professor of political economy and a professor of religious studies. Nor is it a coincidence that Kari and Gregory's acquaintance began with the founding of the Karl Polanyi Institute of Political Economy, where they participate, with many others, in a dialogue on democracy and social justice. What is surely coincidental is that they were born in the same year and only days apart! The publication of this book will be the occasion for a belated celebration of Kari and Gregory's eightieth birthdays, in June 2003.

In preparing this collection, it was striking how the tributes to Kari and Gregory and their own essays provide the foundation for a critical methodology in the humanities and the social sciences. In many ways, they speak with one voice, while drawing upon their respective fields of expertise and engagement. Within the social sciences, the recognition of the need for wider interdisciplinary perspectives in recent years has, in most universities, not had the hoped-for results. Disciplinary divisions remain, dialogue is rare between university departments, the bridge between the humanities and the social sciences has yet to be built. There are some exceptions, especially as the current support for large research teams demands a broader perspective. But the resistance to interdisciplinary scholarship continues. Readers of this volume will have access to scholars who not only crossed disciplinary boundaries long ago but have stepped outside the university to participate in and influence public debate on critical issues for many years. As scholars and activists, as social theorists and engaged intellectuals, Kari and Gregory's writings and public appearances equip a wider audience with analytical tools to challenge prevailing views. This volume is dedicated to Kari Polanyi Levitt and Gregory Baum.

Kari and Gregory have lived parallel lives: their European heritage and emigration to Canada, the years spent in Toronto before settling in Montreal, their active role in Quebec society and in Canadian progressive politics, their years at McGill University, their collaboration through the Polanyi Institute. Both emigrated to England to escape the horrors of fascism. Kari left Vienna in 1934 to join her father in London. She spent the war years in Cambridge and London where she worked in labour research for the Amalgamated Engineering Union before graduating from the London School of Economics with a brilliant first in 1946. The following year she joined her future husband, Joseph Levitt, in Toronto, where she completed graduate studies in economics at the University of Toronto. In 1961 Kari was invited to McGill University as professor of economics. Following her retirement in 1992, she was appointed professor emeritus, economics, McGill University.

Gregory arrived in England from Berlin in 1939, was interned there in 1940 and brought to Canada as an internee, where he was released in 1942. He completed an undergraduate degree in mathematics and physics at McMaster University in Hamilton, Ontario, in 1946 and a master's degree in mathematics at the University of Ohio the following year. His interests then shifted to Christian theology, leading him to pursue doctoral studies at the University of Fribourg, Switzerland, where he received a Ph.D. in theology in 1956. From 1959 to 1986 Gregory was professor of theology and religious studies at St Michael's College, University of Toronto. He then joined McGill University as professor of religious studies until his retirement in 1995. He is currently professor emeritus of theological ethics and sociology of religion, McGill University.

While their personal trajectories did not bring them together until the late 1980s, when they met at McGill University in Montreal, theirs is a common experience of exile and active public engagement in their adopted country. Kari Polanyi Levitt and Gregory Baum have been recognized as remarkable Canadians, as internationally renowned scholars, and as steadfast advocates for democracy and social justice. As political activists, commentators, acclaimed experts, and social critics, they have argued fervently and resolutely against the economism and individualism of the last twenty-five years and in favour of the need to renew progressive politics, while vigorously resisting the pragmatism that such renewal has implied in recent years, as many parties on the left embraced the rhetoric of their opponents to win over the electorate. Their voices are heard in English Canada, in Quebec, and abroad. Inspired by their work, we are better able to argue for social justice, for new socio-economic arrangements, for the alternatives that are now sought by the thousands who are demonstrating against a worldview that privileges markets over people.

Contributors to this volume speak eloquently to the influence Kari and Gregory have had within their respective fields throughout their distinguished careers. Kari taught economic theory and development economics for many years at McGill University and in the Caribbean, at the University of the West Indies. The two worlds to which she has devoted her career, Canada and the Caribbean, are brought together in her book, *Silent Surrender*, first published in 1970. Her detailed analysis of foreign direct investment in Canada had an immediate impact on left intellectuals and within policy circles. We recall the heady debates that followed and the response of the Canadian government in monitoring capital inflows. However, Kari's contribution was far greater. The originality of this book lay in its historical analysis of Canada as a "hinterland economy" and the overseas operations of multinational corporations as vectors of a "new mercantilism." The work was influenced by the staples theory of Harold Innis, by the writings of Latin American structuralists, and by Kari's own work on the plantation economy with her longtime collaborator and friend, Lloyd Best.

Kari's two worlds come together in her writings and public lectures on international development, on the complex issues of international finance and debt. The intellectual influences are the same, enriched by her own contributions over the last thirty years and by a growing number of critical or heterodox economists. Kari has assailed the international community for blackmailing developing countries into adopting suicidal economic strategies and programs. She is now joined by eminent economists such as Joseph Stiglitz in calling for major policy reform at the international level. Kari's numerous essays, articles, and invited lectures in Canada and abroad on the crippling debt crisis in developing countries have not only documented the devastation wrought by years of structural adjustment and conditionality imposed on these vulnerable countries but rigorously argued that the theoretical basis underlying such policies is fundamentally flawed. The world is now aware of social and economic crises induced by these programs; it has yet to acknowledge the bankruptcy of the paradigm that drives these policies. Kari's fascinating critical correspondence with Michael Manley in the 1990s in Jamaica shortly before his death sadly confirm the difficulties faced by progressive thinkers forced to act pragmatically in a world that has made it difficult, if not impossible, to act autonomously and risk political isolation and deeper economic crisis. These debates tell us a great deal about contemporary political economy as a hegemonic discourse governs economic policy regimes internationally in a world as yet unprepared to admit failure, despite mounting evidence.

Both Kari and Gregory have challenged powerful institutions as scholars and as public intellectuals. Tragically, the economics profession resembles the institutional church in its resistance to an alternative discourse. For more than two decades there has been little possibility for debate. The current international revolt by economics students demanding alternative perspectives in their university courses, begun in France in 2001, says a great deal more than we can about the need for debate. And so it is difficult to resist the metaphor of the church in this all too brief summary of the contributions Kari and Gregory have made to intellectual life. They have both fought against powerful forces that have tried to marginalize or silence critical perspectives, that have denigrated a long tradition of radicalism within secular and religious thought.

Gregory Baum's lifelong commitment to social justice led him to challenge the conservative trends in the Catholic Church. His inspiring lectures to several generations of students and social activists, within Christian social movements in Quebec, English Canada, and abroad, represent a powerful counter-movement within Christianity that at once contests the dominant discourse of the institutional churches and celebrates the tradition of prophetic religion that provides a powerful moral, ethical, and religious foundation for social justice. In more than twenty books and hundreds of articles and essays in scholarly journals and the popular press, Gregory has analyzed the "ambiguity of religion," a term he uses to distinguish within religion between the liberating trend that resists injustice and the ideological trend that legitimates the established order. The contradictions in society project themselves into religious thought and practice. The Catholic Church has at times acknowledged this liberating current, most notably in several papal encyclicals and pastoral letters of the Canadian bishops that progressive scholars, both religious and secular, continue to recall as significant statements condemning the oppression of people as a violation of Christian philosophy and ethics. Gregory has contributed significantly to this social movement within the Church. He was prominent during the Second Vatican Council in the 1960s as a theologian on the Secretariat for Christian Unity. Unhappy with the Church's reluctance to change some of its positions, he resigned many years later from the active priesthood, yet he has remained a widely heard theological voice in Catholicism.

As editor of *The Ecumenist*, a critical review of theology, culture, and society, Gregory has generated a dialogue between critical secular and religious thinkers for more than forty years. This conversation distinguishes his own work, intellectually grounded in social theory and Catholic social teaching. Gregory's writings and lectures have radicalized and mobilized intellectuals, students, and activists in their search for social justice, for a universal social ethic. In Quebec, where the Catholic left has a lively tradition of political activism and debate, Gregory is a beacon and an inspiration. As a contributor and member of the editorial board of *Rélations*, the francophone journal of the Jesuit community in Quebec, he has joined a long tradition of critical social thinkers in Quebec who have used this tribune to give voice to an alternative left perspective in this province.

At a time when the world is increasingly divided by race, religion, and ethnicity, Gregory speaks eloquently about the common spirituality that binds world religions together, a spirituality committed to individual and societal freedom. This might ring hollow as we witness human tragedy unfold yet again and as we anticipate more rather than less intolerance of the other. Gregory Baum's writings, his lectures to students, to militants, to the general public, speak to the distortions that betray religions and tear peoples apart by denying their common humanity and spiritual legacy.

Neo-liberal ideology, notwithstanding the numerous and continuous contradictions between its rhetoric and practice, has dominated world politics for almost thirty years. State engagement has actually increased throughout this period; governments have never played a more interventionist role, and non-elected international bodies have exercised extraordinary power, brokering strategies and policies to destroy the social contract in the North and to further condemn the poor nations of the South. Neo-liberalism has claimed several victories: the first and most serious was the dismissal of any alternative strategy as rearguard and unsound. The ideological assault was fierce: even Keynesianism was considered subversive, given the central role it assigns to the state. This is familiar to many readers of this volume but bears repeating to emphasize that the struggle for a progressive alternative had to be waged on two fronts. The first was political. It became exceedingly difficult to present an alternative, as many social democrats capitulated, advocating variants of the so-called "third way," dressing progressive politics in neo-liberal clothes. The second was conceptual. Within critical social thought, the greatest and perhaps unexpected victory of neo-liberalism was the seduction of post-modernism and identity politics that, for some time, demobilized progressive thinkers from constructing a coherent alternative vision, as their now-fragmented theoretical universe paradoxically mirrored their post-modernist view of the world. Kari and Gregory were not seduced. They went on the offensive with many others, distancing themselves from what they saw as fads and as a dangerous retreat from politics that would only further consolidate neo-liberalism, now faced with no coherent opposition. They argued for the need to reconcile identity politics with a larger democratic and societal agenda, insisting that these were not contradictory. They argued passionately against the surrender of the values that must always clearly distinguish progressive politics; against the compromise sought by those who willingly traded electoral victory for democratic renewal.

The years following the dramatic collapse of communism in 1989 and the unfulfilled promise of neo-liberalism as it extended its reach to the former Soviet Union and Eastern and Central Europe are stained by tribal and ethnic wars in the North and in the South; marred by the financial crises in East Asia, Mexico, Brazil, Argentina, and Turkey; and growing disparities between and within the North and the South. It had already become clear that the paradigm dominating the world economy since the mid-1970s was no longer defensible on any grounds in 1998, when we held our conference in honour of Kari and Gregory. One year later, civil society achieved what institutionalized politics had thus far failed to do. Seattle shook the world as thousands of young people poured into the city and prevented the World Trade Organization from holding its scheduled meetings. This was the first of many such demonstrations against world leaders gathered to negotiate the future of the global economy behind closed doors. The anti-globalization movement was born. At the same time, Porto Alegre became the site for the World Social Forum, a counterpoise to the annual meetings by world economic leaders in Davos, Switzerland. The advocates for a globalized market economy now face an organized and articulate resistance movement, a movement that is taken seriously. Environmentalists, anti-sweatshop activists, the women's movement, the labour movement, activists in the social and solidarity economy, and many citizens of the world are not only resisting – they are articulating alternative democratic strategies. The world is paying attention and responding.

The globalization of dissent has shaken the conceit of world leaders. Their stage has transformed dramatically; those in power could not ignore the surge of discontent that spilled into the streets in December 1999 and since. Or so we thought, until September 11th, when the attack on the United States strengthened its grip on the world as it declared "war on terrorism," undermining civil liberties in the name of national security. The contagion spread quickly as other countries, including our own, introduced measures that violate personal freedom. The world was put on hold. The invasion of Afghanistan strengthened U.S. resolve, despite the failure to bring democracy to that beleaguered nation. Its hunt for terrorists shifted the focus of the United States to Iraq and Saddam Hussein's alleged weapons of mass destruction. Shocked at its inability to gain the support of the United Nations Security Council to invade Iraq, the United States responded with insult and indignation. Its growing isolation changed nothing. Nor did large manifestations of public opposition, as millions of people participated in anti-war demonstrations throughout the world. Anti-war protests were expressed through art, through text, through spontaneously organized local events and internationally coordinated gatherings. Over 1,000 theatres around the world opened their doors for free performances of Lysistrata by Aristophanes. Still, the prospect of war with Iraq was transformed into a brutal reality. The United States did not fear the global instability that it unleashed or the force of world opposition.

Today, despite mounting evidence of an unjustified war, the critical U.S. election in the fall of 2004 was fought on the commitment to win the battle against terrorism, justifying whatever means are necessary. This is a tragic moment for democracy. Fundamental processes of dissent and debate are invalidated: not only are oppositional voices discredited but the inability of an independent commission in the U.S. to substantiate the allegations made to justify the invasion of Iraq is being ignored. Nor is the arrogance of the United States shaken by the atrocities and insecurity that are the daily realities of post-war Iraq. Political stability is only in the imaginations of those who take no responsibility for this situation.

Our conference was about "reclaiming democracy," to reflect the ongoing struggle to which Kari Polanyi Levitt and Gregory Baum have dedicated their lives. We could never have imagined the significance of this title at the time, as oppositional voices that are creatively and courageously resisting the suppression of democracy in the interest of security are dismissed or silenced. But peace and security are synonymous with democracy and social justice. The urgency to reclaim democracy has never been greater.

Kari Polanyi Levitt and Gregory Baum eloquently speak to the tributes by their colleagues and friends in their own essays within this volume. They write of the important influences each has had on their scholarship and public lives. Their essays weave these tributes together and in so doing provide a tapestry for the reader, a vibrant and exciting work of scholarship, of memory, of hope. The search for social justice, the need to reclaim democracy, cannot succeed without coherent strategies that draw upon a wide body of knowledge and expertise, popular struggle, and a renewal of those values that have been undermined by a dominant and virulent orthodoxy. This volume raises the issues that have preoccupied Kari and Gregory throughout their professional lives. We must continue to ask the questions addressed in the following chapters, even if we still seek answers. We are grateful to Kari and Gregory for providing the opportunity for this reflection. We are very grateful to the contributing authors for providing the foundation for a new critical analysis. The work that remains to be done is our collective responsibility.

SOCIAL ETHICS AND DEMOCRACY

1 Planning and the Religious Mind; "Der Mensch denkt, Gott lenkt"

URSULA M. FRANKLIN

Please allow me to begin with my thanks – being asked to contribute to this book is a privilege and an expression of friendship that I appreciate deeply. The invitation has also given me the impetus to revisit the issue of planning and think about the inherent ambiguities in its foundation and practice that have troubled me for many years.[1]

The thoughts offered in this paper rest on a few assumptions. One of them is that there are two attributes that seem to differentiate between secular and religious views and value systems. Certainly, these are not *all* the distinguishing attributes, but these two will suffice for the task at hand. The religious mind is informed by the knowledge that *power* is not merely the aggregation of human might (the German *Macht* shows so nicely the link to *machen*, that is the ability to make or to create). All religions stress that there are powers above and beyond human knowledge and interventions. Furthermore, while secular approaches reckon *time* in terms of the life time of individuals or governments, religious faith involves a very different sense of time – and with it a different scale of obligation and stewardship. Next I need to delineate the particular realm of planning that I wish to address because I want to focus on modern planning.

Of course, there have always been prophecies and predictions of the future, based on experiences and observations of the past.[2] The type of planning I want to look at here involves deliberate and organized attempts – *plans* – to structure and design future commercial, social, and political developments. Such private and public planning activities are relatively recent phenomena, made possible – and at times necessary –

by the technological and political changes brought about by and since the Industrial Revolution.

The Industrial Revolution brought new methods of production and factories that utilized new divisions of labour and new prescriptive technologies. These technologies in turn required new and different levels of coordination, planning, and management. The prescriptive technologies and their structures spread well beyond the manufacturing industries, profoundly changing all social and political relations.[3] In the wake of these developments, many social images and metaphors changed. Notions of production, of input-output and efficiency came first to supplement, and then to substitute for, the traditional images of shared experience drawn from nature – metaphors of seed and growth, soil and sea, of bearing fruit and facing decay. The new images conveyed the increasing sense of mastery and control that production technologies – and the new sciences that complemented them – gave to certain people and institutions.

Thus, with the success of industrial manufacturing came the justification of an increasingly secular view of time and power, as well as the acceptance of planning and management as a legitimate commercial and political activity. After the First World War, more and more of the life of a Western nation began to be seen as a production activity – and regulated or planned accordingly. The acceptance of the GNP (the Gross National Product) as an important indicator of a nation's wellbeing symbolizes this mind set. The present economic and political situation of nations, including the effects of globalization, must be seen both as intended and unintentional planning outcomes.[4] In retrospect one may forget how many good and deeply moral people saw efficient and well-planned industrial production as a potential instrument for social justice and human betterment. Some of the best minds of the time enthusiastically urged enlightened planning.[5]

Throughout the first half of the twentieth century and beyond, the scope of and the approach to planning activities appears to be discussed mainly in terms of "who plans for whom." While aims and planning parameters might vary greatly, among, say, planning for corporate expansion, national security, public health or land use, the planning process itself, that is, the laying down of conditions, procedures, and instruments for structuring both present and future endeavours, remained essentially prescriptive, in the sense of industrial production.[6] Thus, even highly motivated and enlightened planners came perilously close to playing God – claiming dominion over the future by attempting to plan it, to "fix it up."

Kenneth Boulding[7] pointed out that while plans and planners are readily accepted, little attention is given to the *plannees*, those who have to conform to the plans of others – like it or not. Yet the success of any and all plans depends significantly on the cooperation and consent of the plannees; the downfall of many plans can be traced to the resistance and creative avoidance schemes of reluctant or unwilling plannees.

Planning, one should not forget, has not always been a good word in Western political discourse. While corporate planning and budgeting were regarded as prudent activities, public and state planning were for a long time synonymous with political coercion and ideological brainwashing. Soviet-style five-year plans were not only criticized as inefficient and simplistic but also as intrinsically oppressive and thus unacceptable tools of a democratic society. We all remember George Orwell's images of conformity as he tried to illustrate the human consequences of being captive plannees.[8] Nevertheless, since the discussions of the 1930s, which were strongly influenced by the events of the Great Depression, thinkers like Gunnar Myrdal have regarded public planning and an increased public sphere as essential components of progressive social policies.[9] But it was *war* that provided the great justification and extension of planning and its tools. Once "total war" became the umbrella that covered a country's directives and plans, attempts at noncompliance by plannees could be readily dismissed as treason.[10] The political and psychological environment of war, with its opportunities to commandeer human and material resources and direct their deployment, led to the development and use of new techniques of management and control in the countries at war. The field of operational research (also called "operations research") may serve as an illustration of the war structure in planning practices.

It is worthwhile to go back to the accounts of one of the field's most foremost British practitioners, Professor P.M.S. Blackett, the 1948 Nobel Laureate in Physics. In his *Studies of War*, he describes the emergence of the science of systemic planning and assessment of war activities.[11] The cool, scientific analysis and evaluation of military operations, together with the single-minded focus on the destructive powers of war forged a set of powerful planning tools; the new quantitative approaches to the efficiency of operations was startling even to the military.

In 1953 Blackett presented his reflections on the problems studied by means of operational research. In his paper, he speaks about his wartime assessment of the "dehousing by bombing of the German working class population" and of his mathematical predictions of the number of civilian casualties resulting from British bombing raids on German cities. He comments, sounding somewhat disappointed, that "the actual number of German civilians killed in 1941 was 200 per month, just one half of my estimate."[12] Rereading Blackett's account today of the debates regarding the bombing of purely civilian targets for the sole purpose of demoralizing the enemy population is interesting in this connection. The discussion shows clearly that those advisors to Whitehall who objected to the practice – be it at the time or later – did so because "it did not work." It did not seem to trouble them that the practice was immoral and illegal; the important facet was that it was inefficient and wasteful of resources. This they demonstrated quantitatively in units of tons of bombs per person killed. It seems as if the commandment "Thou shalt not kill" had been replaced by the dictum "Thou shalt not kill inefficiently."[13]

With these uncommonly transparent arguments, Blackett introduced Operational Research as a new and sophisticated planning tool, well suited to assess the means of war in terms of their quantitative effectiveness. By the end of the war, operational research was regarded as a positive and important new development in the field of planning and management.

Blackett foresaw clearly the subsequent growth of operational research. He wrote in 1948: "Operational Research, the technique of the scientific analysis of operations of war, particularly as developed in Great Britain during the late war, has been the subject of considerable amount of public discussion. The interest in these developments lies partly in the practical importance of the results achieved and partly in the feeling that similar methods might be applied with success to some of the urgent problems of the post war world." Yet, not even Blackett could have foreseen the speed and enthusiasm with which this planning strategy was incorporated into postwar economic and social policy making.[14] The imperative of planning for outcome by the most efficient, though not necessarily the most acceptable means, was smoothly transposed from war to a postwar period, which in turn quickly became a bipolar, cold war world.

While during World War II most plannees accepted the constraints and interventionist measures of wartime planning "for the duration," many of the constraints – such as the quantification of activities, the emphasis on the measurable over the intangible – remained long after the war. The plannee remained to a large extent a servant of plans. While the plans became primarily commercial, the strategies and tactics remained military, including the disregard for plannees and for context. Thus "the war on poverty" hardly considered the views of the poor, and "the war on drugs" rarely dealt with the power plays and the economics of the international drug trade.

As the massive transfer of military technologies to the private and public sector shaped the industrial world, the large-scale use of computers, the development of huge data bases and their interlinking began to turn planning into programming. Tools of unprecedented power became available to the global ruling apparatus and, it seems to me, are being used mainly to turn all of God's world into one giant production site. As citizens and as communities, we are continually forced to be both planners and plannees whether we like it or not. Who among us has not been part of drawing up yet another "strategic plan?" Who has not seen the narrowing of their personal and moral scope as a result of being a multidimensional plannee, a component part of many plans?

All of us are enmeshed, usually without our consent, in schemes of power and dominance, in attempts to predetermine the future. Most of these schemes do not work for any length of time, not even for the powerful, not even for the oppressor. The present, our daily here-and-now is, after all, the recent past's future and in this light it is hard to think of any moral or religious justification for supporting current planning activities. This, then, is the moral and the practical "outch nerve" of the enterprise of planning. Since all present planning (programming, modeling) involves the structuring of the future though technical and social design based on specifying desirable outcomes, *in the production sense of the term*, one has to face the question: Is it morally defensible to participate in a process that "creates" or arranges the future for others? Is such a process practically doable? My own answer is No to both parts of the query as posed.

I would now like to provide the reasons for my stance and suggest another approach to planning that might be more helpful. First, let me focus on the fundamental distinction between *organism* and *mechanism*, a Kantian distinction that Brian Goodwin restated beautifully in a recent book on modern biology:

> A mechanism is a functional unity in which the parts exist for one another in the performance of a particular function (think of the clock and the assembly of its pre-existing parts to serve a dynamic function, i.e., keeping time).
>
> An organism, on the other hand, is a functional *and* structural unity, in which the parts exist for *and by means of* each other, in the expression of a particular nature. This means that the parts of a particular organism – roots, leaves, flowers; eyes, heart, brain – are not made independently and then assembled as in a machine, but arise as a result of interactions within the organism.[15]

Clearly society is an organism and Gregory Baum has reminded us of Karl Polanyi's emphasis on the individual's need and right to be a functional part of society, contributing to its evolution.[16] The methods of industrial planning and management that were derived for the utilization of increasingly complex arrays of mechanisms, may be inherently unsuitable to "manage" organisms. I hold this view, though I am aware of some of the sophisticated attempts to study complexity and self-organizing systems, as well as of the advances in large scale computer modeling.[17] These refinements of planning and programming tools pose special problems for those concerned with justice and with the well being of God's creation: The very sophistication of the instruments can hide the fact that they are still outcome-focused, still based on production thinking. Besides, the development of more and more fancy tools can prolong the temptation to regulate nature and society as if they were manageable mechanisms, while impeding their functioning as evolving organisms.

Let us reaffirm that society is a living organism and that organisms are characterized by their functioning that is, *how* their components work together, and try to draw some conclusions from the mechanism/organism dichotomy. *What if*, for a moment, we were to stop being preoccupied with *what* is to be done, but worry about *how* things are done. In other words, switch the attention from *ends* to *means*, from product to process. Such a shift would recognize the lessons of our daily social reality: that, beyond the world of isolated mechanisms, "outcome" is not really programmable or predictable. (Kenneth Boulding used to speak about the "who-would-have-thought" theory of history). This change of focus would remind us, too, how profoundly the *means* determine the *ends*: Wars do not bring peace; unjust laws cannot advance justice.

A planning shift from ends to means could also facilitate negotiations between planners and plannees. If one could even begin a planning discourse, a discourse about structuring the future, by considerations of means, attention would move away from outcome-related details to the principles of life and community, a realm that does not constrain the religious mind of either the planner or the plannee but could utilize the insights that religious knowledge can provide.

What if one were to look for consensus on the most unacceptable of means? *What if* one would prepare for a future in which killing is unacceptable as a means to any end, however desirable the "outcome" may appear? Since the "Thou shalt not kill" surely includes the killing of spirit and body through deprivation and oppression, considering means that kill as unacceptable could be an effective and universal "means test" for trade deals and for the support of foreign as well as domestic policies. Why not consider, discuss, and teach the "means" option as the planning to plan?

Finally, I see a direct connection between my plea for considering *means* as a planning focus and the work of Gregory Baum. His emphasis on solidarity and on the inclusive nature of community has always been a reminder that the activity of each part of the social organism affects all other parts and is at the same time shaped by them. This implies for Baum a moral obligation toward "the other" as an autonomous partner in community, a partner to be respected and validated.

Maybe watching over the means that a society uses to accomplish its tasks is a useful way to meet this obligation. Maybe it offers a mode of planning that might be practically realizable as well as being acceptable to the religious mind.

NOTES

1 Ursula M. Franklin, "On Speaking Truth to Planning." *Friends Journal* September (1978):6–9.

2 Richard Lewinsohn, *Science, Prophecy and Prediction* (New York: Harper & Brothers, 1961).

3 Ursula M Franklin, *The Real World of Technology* (Toronto: House of Anansi Press, 2nd ed., 1999).

4 See for instance:
Fernand Braudel, *Afterthought on Material Civilisation and Capitalism* (Baltimore: Johns Hopkins University Press,1977).
Michel Chossudrovsky, *The Globalization of Poverty* (Atlantic Highlands NJ: Zen Books, 1997).
William Greider, *One World, Ready or Not* (New York: Simon & Schuster, 1997).
Eric Hobsbawm, *Age of Extremes* (London: Little, Brown, 1994).

5 John Desmond Bernal, *The Social Uses of Science* (London: Routledge, 1939). See also Maurice Goldsmith and Alan Mackay, eds., *The Science of Science, Essays on the Twenty-Fifth Anniversary of the Publication of "The Social Function of Science"* (Harmondsworth: Penguin, 1964).

6 Gunnar Myrdal, *Beyond the Welfare State; Economic Planning and its International Implications* (New Haven and London: Yale University Press, 1960); and Dostaler Gilles, Diane Ethier, and Laurent Lepage, eds., *Gunnar Myrdal and his Work* (Montreal: Harvest House, 1992).

7 Kenneth E. Boulding, "Technology and the Changing Social Order," in David Popenoe, ed., *The Urban Industrial Frontier. Essays in Social Trends and Institutional Goals in Modern Communities* (New Brunswick NJ: Rutgers University Press, 1969); and Kenneth E. Boulding, "Some Reflections on Planning, the Value of Uncertainty," *Technology Review*, MIT, November (1974):1–8.

8 George Orwell, *Nineteen Eighty Four* (London: Secker & Warburg, 1949). See also J.D. Bernal, "The Assessment of Soviet Planning," *Science in History*, 3rd ed., vol. 4. (NY: Penguin, 1965, 1183–93).
9 Myrdal, *Beyond the Welfare State.*
10 For example, consider the treatment of conscientious objectors to war service. For a modern survey, see: Peter Brock, *Twentieth-Century Pacifism* (New York & Toronto: Van Nostrand Reinhold, 1970); and Merja Pentikainen, ed., *The Right to Refuse Military Orders* (Geneva International Peace Bureau, 1994).
11 P.M.S. Blackett, *Studies of War. Nuclear and Conventional.* (New York: Hill and Wang, 1962), particularly Part II: "Operational Research."
12 Blackett, *Studies of War,* 169.
13 *In the current war "plan," the attack on Iraq, "Shock and Awe," is presented as an enormous advance in military precision. The reality of this brutal war has American war experts disturbed by unanticipated resistence and the failure of their "efficient" strategy. One reads these disturbing references by Professor Franklin in a context we could not have predicted.* [Editor's Note]
14 For archetypical examples see for instance: S. Beer, *Decision and Control. The Meaning of Operational Research and Cybernetics* (London and New York: Wiley, 1966); or P. Whittle, *Optimization under Constraints* (London and New York: Wiley, 1971).
15 Brian Goodwin, *How the Leopard Changed its Spots; The Evolution of Complexity* (New York and London: Simon & Schuster, 1994:197).
16 Gregory Baum, *Karl Polanyi on Ethics and Economics* (Montreal and Kingston: McGill-Queen's University Press, 1996).
17 See, for instance: *The Science and Praxis of Complexity* (Tokyo: The United Nations University, 1985), particularly the papers by E. Morin, M. Zeleny, and G.P. Chapman.

2 On Culture, Religion, and Development

DENIS GOULET

For Gandhi, religion and politics are inseparable. "My devotion to Truth," he writes, "has drawn me into the field of politics; and I can say without the slightest hesitation, and yet in all humility, that those who say that religion has nothing to do with politics do not know what religion means."[1] And ever since their founder uttered the curt injunction "Give back to Caesar the things that are Caesar's, and to God the things that are God's,"[2] Christians have been trying to decipher exactly what things belong to God and to Caesar.

"Development" – an image of secure affluence and fulfilling lives for all – is the most potent political myth of the twentieth and the first years of the twenty-first centuries. It has penetrated deeply into all continents. Yet notwithstanding its promise of secular salvation via technological rationality, development has not eliminated religion from the face of the earth. "There are," notes the sociologist Peter Berger, "vast regions today in which modernization has not only failed to result in secularity but has instead led to reaffirmations of religion." Why this "re-enchantment of the world," occurring long after what Max Weber called its "disenchantment" via processes of secularization? The answer may be that:

> Modern scientific thought places man in a universe devoid of supernatural presences and modern technology gives him the limited comfort of increasing his control over the universe, limited because it cannot ever change the root circumstances of human finitude and mortality ... It may be true that the reason

for the recurring human outreach toward transcendence is that reality indeed includes transcendence and that reality finally reasserts itself over secularity.[3]

Berger points to another possibility, "that religious resurgences occur for psychological rather than ontological reasons. Reality is indeed cold and comfortless, but human beings seek comfort and, again and again, they will be prepared to embrace comforting illusions." What is incontrovertible, and important, is the empirical fact: "the recurring human outreach toward transcendence."[4]

The Canadian economist David Pollock asks: "Does man live by GNP alone? ... What are the transcendental values – cultural, ethical, artistic, religious, moral – that extend beyond the current workings of the purely economic and social system?"[5] And Godfrey Gunatilleke, Director of Marga (Sri Lanka Centre for Development Studies) laments that "political and religio-cultural components are not kept in the field of vision of experts and are left outside the development strategy itself." Why this omission, he asks:

> The reluctance of current development thinking to engage in a discussion of these issues ultimately has its roots in a system of cognition, a structure of knowledge which is partial and incomplete. In the development strategies that are propagated it is always the pursuit of material well-being, the socio-economic component of development which has primacy. Underlying this bias are the European ideologies of social change and the cognitive systems which grew out of the industrial revolution and enthroned the economist's view of society and man.[6]

These statements lead us to our question: How do religion, culture, and development impinge on one another? As it is generally conducted, development damages culture and marginalizes religion, substituting in their place a secular culture indifferent to transcendence. This onslaught generates cultural resistance, however, which points to new ways of viewing the relations of culture and religion to development.

CULTURES UNDER ASSAULT

"Culture" is the living sum of meanings, norms, habits, and social artifacts which confer identity on members of some visible community which has its own way of relating to the environment, of identifying insiders and strangers, and of deciding which values are or are not important to it. Essential to any culture are the definitions it makes of its basic needs and its preferred modes of satisfying these. Although it is widely assumed that they are shaped by biological necessities, human needs are to a large extent derived from cultural values. The anthropologist Dorothy Lee explains that needs:

> Are derivative, not basic. If, for example, physical survival was held as the ultimate goal in some society, it would probably be found to give rise to those needs which have been stated to be basic to human survival; but I know of no culture where human physical survival has been shown rather than unquestioningly assumed by social scientists to be the ultimate goal. *I believe that it is value, not a series of needs, which is at the basis of human behavior.* The main difference between the two lies in the conception of the good which underlies them.[7]

The "meaning systems" of societies – their worldviews, philosophies, religions, total web of symbols and myths – have brought to hundreds of millions of their members a sense of identity, an ultimate explanation of the significance of life and death, and an assigned place in the cosmic order of things. Under the banner of development, powerful standardizing forces dilute cultures and relegate them to purely ornamental, vestigial or marginal positions in society. The *first standardizing force* is technology, especially media technology, which operates as a potent carrier of such values as individualism, instant gratification, and consumerism. A *second* standardizing force is the modern state, a political institution which is bureaucratic, centralizing, legalistic, and inclined to assert control over ideas, resources, and "rules of the game" in all spheres of human activity. The *third* standardizing force is the spread of the managerial ethos as the one best way to make decisions, not only in business firms but in all institutions: government agencies, universities, airlines, hospitals, and scientific laboratories.

The very pervasiveness of these standardizing forces, however, gives rise to cultural resistance.[8] Many of the world's cultural communities,[9] especially in developing countries, are religion based. As the political scientist Jeff Haynes explains:

> Ordinary people in the Third World found themselves caught by the desires of their governments to modernize their societies along Western lines while at the same time attempting to retain their long held cultural and religious beliefs at a time of almost unprecedented political, economic and technological change. Historically, such developments were, of course, by no means confined to the Third World. In what is now known as the "developed world" or "the West," a parallel development had taken place since the eighteenth century or earlier, which resulted in people being faced with massive and seemingly inexplicable sudden changes in their lives. During this period of industrialization and state centralization, they naturally struggled to make sense of what was

happening to them. Not infrequently, in pre-modern Europe as much as in the contemporary Third World, the explanations they came up with had a strongly religious form.[10]

The broader question we are exploring – how are culture, religion, and development related? – can be illumined by analyzing how Christianity, the religion of "developed" nations, articulates its vision of that relation, and what directions its own cultural resistance to development's homogenizing forces is taking.

CHRISTIANS AND HISTORICAL TASKS

Today's Christians have no choice but to take history seriously. Theologians as diverse as Bonhoeffer, Rahner, Gutierrez, Congar, Pieris, Baum, and Boff have discredited the God who serves as a crutch for human deficiencies. The challenges of global underdevelopment, the spread of mass technology, and rising demands for total human liberation cannot be met simply by postulating answers in "the next world." But can a Christian labour at historical tasks, the tasks of *this* world with full commitment, while remaining or becoming a religious being? Kolakowski observes that some acts "are either performed completely or not at all. We cannot partially jump from a speeding train, partially marry, partially join an organization, or partially die. Accepting the world is one of those acts which cannot be performed partially."[11] Marx called religion "the opium of the people,"[12] an illusion which turns people's energies away from the tasks of constructing justice and equality in the here and now by projecting their hopes onto an eternal, happy afterlife. Yet Lewis Mumford, commenting wryly on the conditions of proletarian workers in nineteenth-century England, retorts: "Religion ceased in large groups to be the opiate of the poor: indeed the mines and the textile mills often lacked even the barest elements of the older Christian culture: and it would be more nearly true to say that opiates became the religion of the poor."[13] If Christians abandon metahistorical transcendence, however, in order to attend fully to history, do they not thereby betray their religion? The answer seemed obvious to Marx and Engels, who wrote derisively of "a theologian who constantly gives a human interpretation to religious ideas and thereby constantly repudiates his fundamental assumption, the super-human character of religion."[14]

The French theologian of spirituality, René Voillaume, describes:

> The temptation for the Christian to commit himself with his whole being to all sorts of scientific, economic, social and political activities, so as to bring

Christian influence to bear on the structure of tomorrow's world, at the possible cost of reducing Christianity to being no more than the best solution to worldly problems, *de facto*, if not *de jure*, and losing the sense of a spiritual kingdom, of the transcendent nature of Christ's mission, of worship, and of the divine supernatural destiny of all humanity.[15]

Committed Christians recognize the danger, but combat underdevelopment and injustice in this world not primarily in order to win heaven, but because it is an urgent human task worthwhile on its own merits. The cultural resistance of Christians to development's reductionist impulses is, accordingly, two-pronged: a distinctive approach to building history, and giving credible witness to transcendence.

THE "COEFFICIENT OF SECULAR COMMITMENT"

Any religion's success in keeping the door open to transcendence without betraying history depends on its "coefficient of secular commitment,"[16] or what Panikkar calls its "homeomorphic equivalent."[17] Two key arenas can be examined to determine how "serious" is the historical commitment of any religion or, more precisely, of any interpretative stream within a religion.

The first vital arena is the valuation a religion places on earthly existence: is human life simply a *means* to some paradise beyond, or is it an *end*, having intrinsic ontological worth? The Christian philosopher Jacques Maritain, in *Integral Humanism*, first published in 1936, struggled to define a paradigm of humanism which considered triumphs in art, political advance, cultural progress, scientific achievement, and ethical maturation as "infravalent" ends. Infravalent ends are not mere means serving trans-temporal ends: they are goals having their own terminal value, although they rank lower than the supreme ultimate goal, blissful eternal union with an infinitely perfect and loving God. Value is assigned to temporal existence for its own sake, not simply as a stepping-stone to some celestial reward. This perspective summons religious believers to work on behalf of more humane and equitable economic and political structures, not because involvement in these arenas is the precondition for religion or God to triumph, but because that involvement is an urgent human duty bearing on tasks valuable in their own right.

Teilhard de Chardin once compared a contemporary pagan, today's secular humanist, with a "true Christian humanist." The former, he says, loves the earth in order to enjoy it; the latter, *loving it no less*, does so to make it purer and draw from it the strength to escape from it. This escape, however, says Teilhard, is not a flight from reality, but rather the opening or "issue" which alone confers final meaning on the cosmos.[18] For him no pretext, however subtle or "spiritual" it may appear, justifies inertia in religious believers faced with pressing secular tasks to accomplish: knowledge and wisdom to gain, greater justice to forge, creativity to unleash, political solidarity to institute, and comprehensive human development to achieve.

A second arena in which a religion's coefficient of secular commitment may be judged is eschatology – the "last things" or the final destiny of human effort. If gods are seen as dramatic saviours who "bail out humanity" in spite of its crimes and follies, humans will be powerfully motivated to "sin by omission" in the face of their ecological responsibilities, their duty to reduce armaments, their summons to abolish misery. What is crucial, therefore, is the link between religiously inspired commitment to human tasks and the "final redemption," "nirvana" or "absorption into Brahman-Atman." If a religion possesses a high coefficient of insertion in history, the link is intrinsic and essential, not extrinsic or accidental.

Development may be fruitfully conceived as the building of history in ways which leave history itself open to transcendence. In a world of plural religions, philosophies, and modes of knowledge, there exists no single predetermined channel to transcendence. For many millions of religious believers, transcendence points to a life after this life, a universe beyond this material world, which alone confers full and final meaning to human efforts applied to historical tasks. Whether historical life be viewed as a testing ground for separating the virtuous from the wicked, or simply as a tragic confirmation of the finiteness of all material things, what matters most are the precise connections envisaged between this-worldly existence and the transcendent reality which is the object of religious faith. Is transcendence something so qualitatively *other* that nothing accomplished in historical time has any direct or proportionate relationship to the higher values? Or conversely, does one's image of transcendence make of collective human effort in time the very prerequisite of triumphant divine intervention as the final crowning of history? Human effort oriented toward transcendence need not be alienated from human tasks; on the contrary, it can draw from its orientation to a value beyond itself a new dignity, urgency, and depth. To this extent, therefore, transcendence which values human effort as an end is a powerful developmental force, the vector of a high coefficient of secular commitment. Huston Smith distinguishes "this-worldly transcendence" – seeking to go beyond finitude via love, hope, or a commitment to a larger task – from what he terms "ontological transcendence." At issue in the present discussion is ontological transcendence, defined by Smith as:

Transcendence deriving from the possibility that reality houses reservoirs of value qualitatively different from what we normally perceive or assume. To pursue the possibility of Ontological Transcendence is, of course, to fly in the face of recent "secular theology," but this pursuit requires no apology. The secular theologians' request that we stop speaking of God as "out there" may be useful, for geography never applies literally to spiritual affairs. But their proposal that we drop all talk of a "behind the scenes" reality seems curious. Secular theologians tend to be science enthusiasts, yet "behind the scenes" sounds like precisely what the scientists have been uncovering as they penetrate deeper and deeper into nature's undersurface.[19]

An additional distinction imposes itself here: that between secularization and secularism. *Secularization* is the process whereby this-worldly values are increasingly taken as decisive in human affairs and as meriting the full energies and attentions of societies' members. *Secularism*, in contrast, is a philosophical stance – whether theoretical or practical – which reduces the world of values or of worthwhile human pursuits to secular matters. The Christian religions endorse the secularization process while rejecting secularism.[20] These distinctions help explain how religions confront development.

RELIGION AND AUTHENTIC DEVELOPMENT

Development generates value conflicts over the meaning of the good life. In Ursula K. LeGuin's science fiction novel *The Dispossessed*,[21] two models of organizing society for promoting the good life vie for the loyalties of people. One model prizes collaboration, friendship, and a high degree of equality, achievable in an austere communitarian regime of disciplined resource use. The other prizes material comfort, individual selfishness, and competition, with its attendant inequalities; it depends on abundant resources.

A second value conflict bears on the foundations of justice and legitimacy in society. Do these rest on inherited authority, the rule of the majority, a social contract? Do political rights and individual freedoms enjoy primacy over collective social and economic rights aimed at assuring that needs are met and that society's common good is served?

A third set of value conflicts centres on the criteria a society adopts to frame its stance toward nature. Is nature viewed simply as raw material for Promethean exploitation by humans, or as the larger womb of life in which humans live, move, and have their being, and whose rhythms and laws they must respect? Should the human stance toward nature be extractive and manipulative or harmony seeking? Providing satisfactory conceptual, institutional, and behavioural answers to these questions constitutes authentic development.

A lifelong study of social theory and clinical observation led the psychologist Erich Fromm to conclude that societies possess a *social character* formed from "the blending of the individual psychical sphere and the socioeconomic structure."[22] It is the "'religious' impulses," he adds, that "contribute the energy necessary to move men and women to accomplish drastic social change, and hence, that a new society can be brought about only if a profound change occurs in the human heart – if a new object of devotion takes the place of the present one."[23]

That object of devotion is development centred on the primacy of *being* over *having*.

The alternative of *having* over *being* does not appeal to common sense. *To have*, so it would seem, is a normal function of our life: in order to live we must have things. Moreover, we must have things in order to enjoy them. In a culture in which the supreme goal is to have – and to have more and more – and in which one can speak of someone as "being worth a million dollars," how can there be an alternative between having and being? On the contrary, it would seem that the very essence of being is having; that if one *has* nothing, one *is* nothing.

Yet the great Masters of Living have made the alternative between having and being a central issue of their respective systems. The Buddha teaches that in order to arrive at the highest stage of human development, we must not crave possessions. Jesus teaches: "For whosoever will save his life shall lose it; but whosoever will lose his life for my sake, the same shall save it. For what is a man advantaged, if he gain the whole world, and lose himself, or be cast away?" (Luke 9:24–25) Master Eckhart taught that to have nothing and make oneself open and "empty," not to let one's ego stand in one's way, is the condition for achieving spiritual wealth and strength. Marx taught that luxury is as much a vice as poverty and that our goal should be to *be* much, not to *have* much. (I refer here to the real Marx, the radical humanist, not to the vulgar forgery presented by Soviet communism.)

For many years, I had been deeply impressed by this distinction and was seeking its empirical basis in the concrete study of individuals and groups by the psychoanalytic method. What I saw has led me to conclude that this distinction, together with that between love of life and love of the dead, represents the most crucial problem of existence; that empirical anthropological and psychoanalytic data tend to demonstrate that *having and being are two fundamental modes of experience, the respective strengths of which determine the differences between the characters of individuals and various types of social character.*[24]

Authentic development means that a society provides, in the *being* mode, optimal life sustenance, esteem, and freedom to all its members. The destruction of life giving resources – thereby operating exclusionary and disparity-inducing economic systems – and the indiscriminate adoption of technologies which destroy human freedoms or close off transcendence constitute not authentic but spurious development. Spurious development breeds opposition, however: it is self-destructive and, ultimately, it cannot be sustained.

Sustainability is needed in five domains: economic, political, social, cultural, and environmental. Long-term economic and environmental viability requires using resources in a way which does not irreversibly deplete them. Political viability rests on creating for all members of society a stake in its survival: this cannot be achieved unless all enjoy freedom and inviolable personal rights and believe that the political system within which they live pursues some common good and not mere particular interests. Finally, if development is to be socially and culturally sustainable, the foundations of community and symbolic meaning systems must be protected. Otherwise, they will be steamrolled into oblivion under the pretext of submitting to the requirements of scientific and technological "rationality."

When they engage development, religions usually promote, in diverse modal specifications, alternative development strategies. Such strategies favour patterns of economic production centring on basic needs, job-creation (largely through the adoption of appropriate technologies),[25] decentralized public infrastructure investment to produce regional and sectoral equity, an adequate social allocation ratio of public expenditures devoted to what the UNDP calls "human priority concerns,"[26] incentives policies[27] favouring increased productivity in low-productivity sectors, and selective linkage and de-linkage with global markets.

CONCLUSION

Religions must avoid two kinds of alienation: a flight from history in which mystery and transcendence become illusions buttressing alienation from historical time, and a flight from transcendence in which religion becomes but a limp surrogate for full secular commitment to history. Religions must accept living in a state of dialectical tension between immanence and commitment on the one hand, and transcendence and detachment on the other.

Religion's most important mission, however, as it confronts the realities of development, is to keep hope alive. By any rational calculation of future probabilities, the development efforts of most countries are doomed to fail. The poor can never catch up with the rich – classes, nations, and individuals – as long as these continue to consume wastefully and to devise ideological justifications for not practising solidarity with the needy. Technological and resource gaps will, in all probability, continue to widen, and vast resources will continue to be devoted to destructive armaments. In any plausible scenario projected over the next fifty years, development remains the privilege of the relatively few, while underdevelopment is the lot of the vast majority. Only some hope that goes beyond rationality, beyond apparent possibility, can elicit the creative energies and vision which authentic development for all requires. Jacques Ellul argues the need for hope in a time of abandonment,[28] and warns humans not to count on a *Deus ex machina* salvation from whatever gods they believe in. Only the human race can extricate itself from the nuclear, ecological, economic, and political impasses it has itself created. Human beings will despair of even attempting to create a wisdom to match their sciences, however, says Ellul, unless they have hope, and grounds for hope, in some God who has entrusted the making of history to them.

Religiously grounded hope finds some measure of scientific validation from the sociobiologist René Dubos, who observes that only a tiny fragment of human brain-power has been utilized up until the present.[29] Hence Africans, Asians, and Latin Americans are capable of inventing new, and more authentic, models of development: they need not be mere consumers of a single pattern of modern civilization in order to be "developed." Religion pleads normatively for a certain reading of history, one in which human agents are makers of history even as they bear witness to transcendence.[30] The most important banner religion must raise is that of hope in the ability to create new possibilities for development.

NOTES

1 Mohandas K. Gandhi, *An Autobiography, the Story of My Experiments With Truth* (Boston: Beacon Press, 1957):504.
2 Matt. 22:21; Mark 12:17.
3 Peter L. Berger, *A Far Glory: The Quest for Faith in an Age of Credulity* (New York: Free Press/Macmillan, 1992):28–9.
4 Ibid:30.
5 David H. Pollock, "A Latin American Strategy to the Year 2000: Can the Past Serve as a Guide to the Future?" Latin American Prospects

for the 80s: What Kinds of Development? Vol. 1, p. 9. Norman Patterson School of International Affairs, Carleton University.

6 Godfrey Gunatilleke, "The Interior Dimension," *International Development Review* 21, no. 1 (1979): 4.

7 Dorothy Lee, *Freedom and Culture* (New Jersey: Prentice Hall, 1959):72. Emphasis in the original.

8 Cultural resistance in several continents is analyzed and illustrated in *The Futures of Culture* (Paris: UNESCO, 1994).

9 The term "cultural communities" is preferable to "cultures." The latter term evokes something abstract, the former suggests living societies animated by their values.

10 Jeff Haynes, *Religion in Third World Politics* (Boulder, CO: Lynne Rienner Publishers, 1994):2.

11 Leszek Kolakowski, "Ethics Without a Moral Code," *Tri Quarterly*, No. 22 (Fall 1971):153.

12 Karl Marx, "Introduction." *Critique of the Hegelian Philosophy of Right* (1844).

13 Lewis Mumford, *Technics and Civilisation* (New York: Harcourt Brace, 1934):179.

14 Lloyd D. Easton and Kurt H. Guddai, eds., "The Holy Family" in *Writings of the Young Marx on Philosophy and Society* (New York: Anchor, 1967):363.

15 René Voillaume, *Au Cœur des Masses* (Paris: Cerf, 1965):532. Author's translation.

16 Denis Goulet, "Secular History and Teleology," *World Justice*, 8, no. 1 (September 1966):5–18.

17 Raimundo Panikkar, "Is the Notion of Human Rights a Western Concept?" *Interculture*, 82 (January–March 1984):28–47.

18 M.B. Madaule, "La personne dans la perspective Teilhardienne," in *Essais sur Teilhard de Chardin*, Collective editors (Paris: Fayard, 1962):76.

19 Huston Smith, "The Reach and the Grasp: Transcendence Today," in Herbert W. Richardson and Donald R. Cutler, eds., *Transcendence* (Boston: Beacon Press, 1969):9.

20 On this see A.T. van Leeuwen, *Prophecy in a Technocratic Era* (New York: Charles Scribner's, 1968):56–67.

21 Ursula LeGuin, *The Dispossessed* (New York: Avon Books, 1975):20.

22 Erich Fromm, *To Have or To Be?* (New York: Harper & Row, 1976):133. An earlier development of the notion of *social character* is found in Erich Fromm and Michael Maccoby, *Social Character in a Mexican Village* (Englewood Cliffs, NJ: Prentice-Hall, 1970).

23 Ibid.

24 Ibid:15–16. Emphasis in the original.

25 How technologies favour, or impede, employment creation is analyzed in Raphael Kaplinski, *The Economies of Small, Appropriate Technology in a Changing World* (London: Appropriate Technology International, 1990).

26 United Nations Development Programme, *Human Development Report 1991* (New York: Oxford University Press, 1991):5–6.

27 Denis Goulet, *Incentives for Development, the Key to Equity* (New York: Horizons, 1989).

28 Jacques Ellul, *Hope in a Time of Abandonment* (New York: Seabury Press, 1973). CF. Lamar Carter, Ann Mische and David R. Schwartz, eds., *Aspects of Hope. The Proceedings of a Seminar on Hope.* New York: ICIS Center for a Science of Hope, 1993.

29 René Dubos, *Man Adapting* (New Haven: Yale University Press, 1978). On efforts to establish a "science of hope" on empirical grounds, see Carter, Mische and Schwartz, eds., *Aspects of Hope.*

30 Denis Goulet, *A New Moral Order* (Maryknoll, NY: Orbis Books, 1974):109–42.

3 On Human Dignity and Human Rights: Western or Universal

ARVIND SHARMA

Human dignity and human rights are two concepts which are often invoked together, as in the very preamble to the Universal Declaration of Human Rights.[1] The relationship between the two, however, remains to be fully clarified. It might well be possible to configure them in several different yet equally credible ways. This is an issue that has political implications since it raises the question whether human rights can claim to be universal or whether they are simply a set of values proper to a particular culture. Can the world religions acknowledge human rights? These are questions I have often discussed with Gregory Baum, my colleague at McGill University.

In the 1990s, I participated in a series of conferences on human dignity and human rights organized by the Pacific Basin Research Center at the John F. Kennedy School of Government at Harvard University. One of my academic interests over the last years has been the meaning of human dignity and the affirmation of human rights in Hinduism and the other Asian religions. At the Pacific Basin conferences, the participants were, with few exceptions, professors in various divisions of Harvard University, most of them secular scholars with no religious affiliation. Harvard Divinity School was represented by Harvey Cox.

Why were these conferences organized by the Pacific Basin Research Center? Since the Western human rights discourse cannot easily be assimilated in Asian cultures, the effort to translate human rights concerns into a discourse on human dignity may open the door to a wider acceptance of these concerns in the Asian religious traditions.

In this paper I shall analyze the discussions that took place at these conferences and explore the relationship between human dignity and human rights as seen by the participants. The paper also refers to a number of unpublished texts that were distributed at the conferences and to additional thinkers from India.

This paper consists of six parts: the first part discusses some definitions of human dignity; the second part examines the relationship between human dignity and rights; in part three the relationship between the two will be assessed in terms of their differences; the fourth part prioritizes human dignity and human rignts in terms of each other in order to further explore the relationship; the fifth part provides historical perspectives on the concept of dignity; and part six attempts to evolve an agenda for future research.

HUMAN DIGNITY: DEFINITIONS

Although both the terms "human rights" and "human dignity" possess that ambiguity which characterizes such key axiological terms, the connotation of the term human rights may be said to be clearer, given the various human rights documents which profess to embody it.[2] I shall therefore focus here only on definitions of human dignity.

On the basis of the discussion of these terms among several scholars and in related literature, the following definitions of human dignity may be identified, along with the names of the scholars to whom they could be attributed:

1 Individual moral self-fulfillment (Montgomery)[3]
2 Dignity involves foregoing an interest or advantage or pleasure because you think it does not comport with your sense of worth ... What one could refuse to do because one is a human being. (Mansfield)[4]
3 [Dignity] should include the idea that there are certain things that could not be done to the individual by anyone, including a government. (Cox)[5]
4 Efforts to define human dignity should begin by articulating such concrete goods as that which government can provide to people to maximize benefits of formal rights. This might encompass basic education, basic health care, and political rights. The positive goods government should provide so that individuals can make the most of their negative liberties or formal rights. (Applebaum)[6]
5 Indeed, respect of persons may simply be respect for their rights, so that there cannot be the one without the other; and what is called "human dignity" may be the recognizable capacity to assert claims. (Fernberg)[7]

These definitions of human dignity notably avoid any reference to the sacred. They remain within the empirical human realm accessible to all, in the hope of arriving at a universally acceptable discourse.

HUMAN DIGNITY AND HUMAN RIGHTS: CONVERGENCES

Areas of overlap between human dignity and human rights can be readily identified in the growing literature on the subject. The views of the following scholars, when pressed to their logical conclusion, point to the potential for convergence between the two concepts.

1 Frederich Schauer[8] draws a distinction between human rights in an ontological sense and positive rights as created by law.[9] In that case, human rights in the ontological sense come very close to, and some may claim actually coincide with, the concept of human dignity.
2 Stephen Holmes argues that rights contain a basis for protection against indignities. Consequently, it might be wrong to characterize dignity as something higher, separate from or beyond rights.[10] Even if one were still to insist that human dignity conceptually differs from human rights, their intimate overlap would be difficult to deny from such a perspective.
3 Samuel H. Beer cites that the distinction between positive and negative rights may be relevant in this context, with dignity comprehending positive rights.[11] Once again almost half of human rights, as it were, become virtually coterminous with human dignity.
4 Joel Feinberg similarly suggests a deep connection between human rights and human dignity, not partially but as a whole, when he writes: "Having rights enables us to "stand up like men," to look others in the eye, and to feel in some fundamental way the equal of anyone. To think of oneself as the holder of rights is not to be unduly but properly proud, to have the minimal self-respect that is necessary to be worthy of love and esteem of others."[12]
5 Joseph Prabhu[13] highlights the close connection between human rights and human dignity, yet recognizes a certain difference between them: "Human rights are the most general sorts of rights, created by the mere fact of being human, as against the more particular cases of civil rights, constitutional rights, municipal rights, etc., which are created by specific contracts or institutions. The predicate 'human,' however, is not so much a naturalistic as a moral predicate, so that what is being referred to in the notion of human rights is not the mere species character of *homo sapiens*, but rather the *dignity of a human being*."[16]

HUMAN DIGNITY AND HUMAN RIGHTS: DIVERGENCES

Just as similarities between human dignity and human rights sometimes stand out, the differences between the two also strike the investigator. The following five scholars, for instance, seem to draw a distinction without necessarily implying a separation.

1 Harvey C. Mansfield notes that "rights are less universal [than dignity] because of their specific origin, but also more universal because they derive from the nature of human beings", while "every culture has some notion of dignity ... Dignity is that way more universal than rights, but also less uniform." He offers another basis for distinguishing between the two when he states that "policies directed toward the protection of rights have an inherent limitation to them, but those directed to the promotion of human dignity do not."[15]
2 John D. Montgomery, like Harvey C. Mansfield, distinguishes between the two in terms of policy. According to him rights policies are "protective" while dignity policies are "generative."[16]
3 Harvey G. Cox regards dignity as underlying human rights. "The dignity element [is] continuous," while human rights can be fought for and obtained incrementally, as, for instance, in the civil rights struggles of the 1960s.[17]
4 Timothy C. Weiskel regards the historical identification of rights with dignity as a passing phase since in the future rights will be claimed not only for humans but also for animals and the natural environment.[18]

HUMAN DIGNITY AND HUMAN RIGHTS: PRIORITIZING DIGNITY

There is a marked tendency in the literature to prioritize dignity. The following scholars prominently manifest this tendency:

1 Stephen Holmes states that "rights are always formulated in a 'yes-but' pattern, [while] human dignity does not build in this limitation." Moreover, "rights are ways that [regulate] our conflicts. They are not a solution to conflicts and they do not offer final ends," whereas dignity might.[19]
2 John D. Montgomery maintains that human rights "is a non-starter in the context of Asia and the Pacific ... Human dignity can be deeply supported in a cross-cultural context," unlike human rights.[20]
3 While Joel Feinberg seems to hesitate on the point, the Indian religious philosopher Rama Rao Pappu uses him as a stepping stone to come

out on the side of human dignity by also linking it with human obligations. He writes:

> If [as J. Feinberg maintains] human rights "enable us to stand up like men ... and to feel in some fundamental way the equal of anyone," human obligations enable us to care, to show concern for other human and sub-human creatures and to bow one's head at the majesty of the moral law and the moral agency which each individual embodies in himself. Likewise, if human rights make us think of ourselves as "properly proud, to have that minimal self-respect that is necessary to be worthy of love and esteem of others, human obligations enable us to think of ourselves as persons having humility, self-discipline and simply be the recognizable capacity to assert claims," we may add that human dignity is not exhausted by the assertion of claims, but should also consist in leading a virtuous life, by discharging one's duties and obligations sincerely and cheerfully.[21]

HUMAN DIGNITY AND HUMAN RIGHTS: PRIORITIZING RIGHTS

John D. Montgomery distinguishes between human rights (which require protection) and human dignity (which requires affirmation). Although he regards dignity as a broader concept than rights,[22] it is clear from his writings that human rights for him constitute a necessary, if not a sufficient, condition for human dignity. In this sense rights can be prioritized over dignity.

THREE WAYS TO LOOK AT HUMAN DIGNITY

Three broad historical perspectives can be identified in the discussion of human dignity in the documents that relate it to human rights. These three perspectives could be called transformational, developmental, and anticipatory.

1 Arthur Applebaum seems to offer a *transformational* perspective of human dignity. "Honour was the old way of understanding dignity ... the shift to a modern democratic [society] involves moving from honour to respect, or from shame to guilt."[23] It is a point worth pondering whether such respect includes respect for rights.
2 Samuel H. Beer interweaves human dignity and human rights from a *developmental* perspective rather than a transformational one. "Human dignity covers a new kind of rights, which came into being in the modern political arena with the advent of the welfare state,

the managed economy and socialism ... The rights concept is very modern and the idea that governments have an obligation to positively generate policies of human dignity even more so."[24]

3 Timothy C. Weiskel offers an *anticipatory* perspective on human dignity, which makes its association with human rights transitional in nature: "The notion of dignity being associated with individual rights (such as the right to non-interference from the state in personal life)" is "a historically conditioned moment," while in the future "categorical demands will be made upon the state to provide rights to basic human amenities" such as water or food, thus limiting personal freedoms.[25]

HUMAN DIGNITY AND HUMAN RIGHTS: AN AGENDA

One may, in conclusion, identify the various suggestions regarding future directions such studies as this one might take.

1 Fredrich Schauer recommends that "particular conceptions of dignity may be evaluated with respect to the degree to which [they] may be more or less efficacious in changing existing conditions." In such a context the concept of progress may be articulated as follows: "Progress is dealing with a set of problems which are more manageable and desirable than the set of problems in the past."[26]

2 F. Schauer also recommends finding "projects that identify ideas of human dignity or rights (...both empirical and philosophical)."[27]

3 John D. Montgomery proposes "research that examines how each of the major religions of Asia and the Pacific would conceive of [moral?] self-fulfilment."[28]

4 Arthur Applebaum proposes dignity-impact studies, analogous to environmental-impact studies.[29]

5 S. Rama Rao Pappu proposes a universal declaration of human rights and obligations for the following four reasons: First, the "Universal Declaration of Human Rights and Obligations," as we may call this, will give us a comprehensive and synthetic view of our conception of human dignity, assimilating the insights of East and West, tradition and modernity. The divisions of mankind living either in a world of rights or in a world of obligations will thereby be broken and the best from both worlds can be integrated.

Second, because the world of obligations is wider than the world of rights, many important features of human dignity and human intercourse which were not included in the current human rights discussion could be easily accommodated. For example, the current human rights doctrines do not include such important moral values like "truth telling," "promise keeping," "alleviating suffering," and so on. The main reason for not including these values seems to be that they do not neatly fit into the "rights doctrines," (e.g., the right to keep one's promises sounds odd). On the other hand, it is clear how impoverished human beings would be without these values. Many of these important values could now be accommodated under the rubric of "human obligations."

Third, the current controversy over whether economic and welfare rights can be properly called "human rights" may also be solved. Since many of the economic rights cannot, under the present economic circumstances of most developing nations, be implemented anyway, we do not gain anything by calling them "human *rights*." On the other hand, by making them "human obligations," individuals and groups do not make empty claims on each other. They could rather think of these as mutuality of obligations whereby everyone has the obligation to promote economic prosperity.

Finally, the very comprehensiveness of the "Universal Declaration of Human Rights and Human Obligations" theory would allow for greater diversity among peoples and nations, so that we do not judge whether a society or a nation is "pro-human rights" by only taking into consideration a country's implementation of, say, "liberty rights" or "personal rights."

Even in contemporary India, for example, the family, the caste and the village look after the welfare and security of the sick, the old, the handicapped and the unemployed as a matter of obligation and this system of obligations seems to work better than systems where the current human rights doctrine of welfare rights are legislated.[30]

6 Ninian Smart and Shivesh Thakur examine how different traditions may arrive at a common understanding while fully recognizing and respecting the different routes toward this understanding. An intriguing question arises as to whether differing cultures can arrive at a similar conclusion about rights by rather different routes – some via explicit philosophizing, as with Locke, Kant, and others in the West; others by contemplating religious texts and duties (the Mimamsa and the *Gita*); others again by exploiting ideas of ritual and performative behaviour towards others (e.g. *li* in China as a source of rights). It would be a happy outcome if so, since it would allow a confluence model of world society to establish itself – differing civilizations like so many rivers coming together, the reverse of a delta.[31]

7 The Philippine scholar, E.E. Lamberte, however, reminds us how deep these differences are. Is there an absolute definition of human rights? Human rights seem to be culturally bound. In Asia, for example, the good of the group transcends that of the individual. There is always a strain between community values and individual values. What is good for us is defined by the culture and institution itself. Intervention is always seen with skepticism in the East, because the framework in the West is based on individuals, whereas in the East the community supersedes the individual. Can we respect a nondemocratic regime that responds to the basic needs of its people? On what basis do we intervene? On what do we base our definition of human rights? We know the idea comes from tradition and religion.[32]
8 Dennis Rondinelli of the Pacific Basin Research Center Rim refers to Huston Smith's argument in *The Religions of Man* that all religions basically teach a certain set of fundamental tenets, one of which is that we treat others as we wish to be treated. Is that accurate, and if so, does this give us some guidelines about how any major religion guides our understanding of basic human rights, or basic human dignity?[33]
9 The very pursuit of human rights could generate human rights abuses and thus compromise human dignity. John D. Montgomery notes the possibility that "wealth protected by the right to property can be used to disadvantage people." Similarly, civil society plays a major role in maintaining human dignity. If the legalization of human rights leads to an erosion of the buffer between people and government provided by [civil society], it may have adverse consequences for human dignity.[34]

CONCLUSION

The Pacific Basin Research Center conferences revealed a certain consensus on human rights and human dignity in the academic disciplines of political philosophy, law, history, sociology, anthropology, and environmental science. This provides a basis for creating a human rights discourse that is all-embracing and nondivisive. As yet no equivalent consensus exists on human rights and human dignity among the religious traditions. At this time relating human rights discourse to the sacred is divisive, because it relies on concepts to which some Asian traditions are unable to be receptive. Yet the research to date is encouraging. The suggestion made by Ninian Smart and Shivesh Thakur that the world religions may come to a consensus regarding human rights, where each defends these rights with different sets of arguments derived from their own religious tradition, is very fruitful. It is here that we need further research. What we search for is an agreement on human rights that honours the cultural and religious pluralism of humanity.

NOTES

1 See *Twenty-Five Human Rights Documents* (New York: Columbia University Press, 1994):6.
2 "Policies in Support of Human Rights and Human Dignity." Pacific Basin Research Centre, Harvard University. Transcript of Proceedings, 3. This unpublished text of thirty pages will subsequently be referred to as *Transcript.*
3 John D. Montgomery, Ford Foundation Professor, Emeritus, International Studies, Kennedy School of Government, Harvard University, *Transcript*, 3.
4 Harvey C. Mansfield, William R. Kenan Jr Professor of Government, Department of Government, Harvard University, Ibid., 3.
5 Harvey G. Cox, Victor S. Thomas Professor of Divinity, Harvard Divinity School, Ibid., 3.
6 Arthur Applebaum, J. F. Kennedy School of Government, Harvard University, Ibid., 3.
7 Joel Feinberg, Philosophy and Law, Harvard University. Cited in S.S. Rama Rao Pappu, "Human Rights and Human Obligations," unpublished paper, 21.
8 Frederich Schauer, Professor of the First Amendment, John F. Kennedy School of Government, Harvard University, *Transcript*, 2.
9 *Transcript*, 2.
10 Stephen Holmes, Professor of Law and Political Science, New York University, Ibid., 5.
11 Samuel H. Beer, Eaton Professor of the Science of Government, Emeritus, Harvard University, Ibid., 4.
12 Pappu, "Human Rights and Human Obligations," 21.
13 Joseph Prabhu, Former Fellow, Harvard Center for the Study of World Religions.
14 Joseph Prabhu, "Dharma as an Alternative to Human Rights," in *Studies in Orientology*, ed. S.K. Maity, Upendra Thakur and A.K. Narain (Agra, India: Y.K. Publishes, 1988):175. Emphasis added.
15 *Transcript*, 6.
16 Ibid., 2.
17 Ibid., 4.
18 Timothy C. Weiskel, Director, Harvard Seminar on Environmental Values, Harvard University Center for the Environment, Ibid., 18–19.
19 Ibid., 6.

20 Ibid., 7.
21 Pappu, "Human Rights and Human Obligations," 24–5.
22 John D. Montgomery, "Human Rights as Human Values," in John D. Montgomery, *Human Rights: Positive Policies in Asia and the Pacific Rim* (Hollis, NH: Hollis Publishing Company, 1998):5.
23 *Transcript*, 4.
24 Ibid., 4, 9.
25 Ibid., 18–19.
26 Ibid., 6.
27 Ibid., 17.
28 Ibid., 17.
29 Ibid., 16–18.
30 Rama Rao Pappu, "Human Rights and Human Obligations," 25–6.
31 Ninian Smart and Shivesh Thakur, eds., *Ethical and Political Dilemmas of Modern India* (New York: St Martin's Press, 1993):xi.
32 Pacific Basin Research Center Retreat, September 30, 1994, 9. An unpublished paper of 23 pages. Subsequently cited as *Retreat.*
33 *Retreat*; Huston Smith, *The Religions of Man.* (New York: Harper, 1958):11.
34 Ibid., 16–19, 21–3.

4 To Build a Just Society: The Catholic Left in Quebec

CAROLYN SHARP

Among Gregory Baum's numerous contributions to theology is that he has taught us to think politically about matters of faith. From his work and his example, we have learned that affirmations of faith, theological discussions, ecclesial structures, and liturgical practices exist not in a vacuum but in given social and political contexts. He has thus challenged us to reflect critically upon the consequences of what we believe and how we live out our faith, in order to free our theologies and our churches from complicity with the forces of oppression and engage these same theologies and churches in the cause of society's most vulnerable members.

Throughout the years, Gregory Baum has maintained ties with the Catholic left in Quebec, recognizing it as a vital force for social change, often taking up his pen to chronicle its evolution.[1] Since moving to Quebec in 1986, he has been a powerful and generous intellectual presence in these circles. He is a dedicated member of the editorial board of *Rélations*, the Montreal-based Jesuit monthly, to which he contributes regularly. He also teaches adult education courses at the downtown Centre Saint-Pierre, is an active participant in the organization of *Les journées sociales,* a biannual gathering of progressive Catholics, and is remarkably available to participate in workshops not only as a speaker and expert but also as a listener and learner. His theological and sociological insight has enriched the life of the Québec Church, most especially its progressive wing.

A PORTRAIT OF THE CATHOLIC LEFT IN QUÉBEC

The primarily Catholic Christian left in Québec consists of a loose network of individuals, groups, and organizations dedicated, in the name of the Gospel, to solidarity with the poor, to social transformation, and to the construction of an alternative social project.[2] Its vision and praxis are, as Baum has noted, pluralistic and shaped by the concrete social struggles in which it is immersed.[3] A dozen or so formal organizations with a variety of focuses exist at the national or Québec-wide level. Development and Peace, Jeunesse du monde, and Entraide missionaire all work in the area of international solidarity and development education. Human rights are the focus of the Association chrétien pour l'abolition de la torture and the Comité chrétien pour les droits humains en Amérique latine. Groups working on women's issues include L'Autre parole, Femmes et ministères and the Réseau œcuménique des femmes. The Centre de pastorale en milieu ouvrier, the Journées sociales and the Centre justice et foi are involved in grass-roots education and provide forums for doing social analysis. Four Catholic Action movements continue to work among students and working-class Christians, the Jeunesse ouvrière chrétienne, the Jeunesse étudiante chrétienne, the Mouvement des travailleurs chrétiens, and the Mouvement des étudiants chrétiens. The Jesuit monthly *Rélations* as well as the magazine *Recto-Verso*, formerly *Vie ouvrière*, work in the field of publications. Moreover, in various cities and regions throughout Québec, there exist similar local organizations such as the Carrefour de pastorale en milieu ouvrier (CAPMO) in Québec City, the English-speaking Social Action Committee or the Bureau chrétien de la communauté haïtienne in Montréal.

It would be, however, inaccurate to restrict an understanding of the Christian left to formal organizations. Throughout Québec, several dozen informal groups meet on a regular basis for various forms of fellowship. Hard to count, some of these groups have existed for twenty years or more, while others last a few years until their members move on to other commitments or at times leave Church connections behind them. Moreover, individual activists self-identify as left-wing Christians, whether or not they have any regular connections with formal Church structures. Such individuals are present in various unions, community organizations, in the women's movement, and in international solidarity groups. These activists may see their social commitment as the primary expression of their faith, while parish attendance or other liturgical practices are quite peripheral to their lives.

Over the past thirty years, a number of national gatherings have allowed this network of organizations, informal groups, and individuals to consolidate its links. The Colloquium organized by the magazine *Dossier "vie ouvrière"* and the Politisés chrétiens, at Cap-Rouge near Québec City, in 1974, are generally recognized as having marked a turning point in the Catholic left's acceptance of radical social analysis and its adoption of a theological framework grounded in liberation theology. From the late seventies through the early nineties, the Centre de pastorale en milieu ouvrier (CPMO) organized a series of colloquia on themes of interest to those Christians involved in grass-roots community organizations. Similarly, the *Entraide missionnaire* holds yearly colloquia on international development questions. In 1989 the Carrefour de pastorale en monde ouvrier (CAPMO) and the Faculty of Theology of Laval University joined together to mark the centenary of *Rerum Novarum* and thus gave birth to the biannual *Journées sociales.*[4] These gatherings easily bring together 300 to 600 participants.

While tensions have marked the relationship between the Catholic left and the institutional Church, it would be wrong to suggest that this movement is strictly extra-institutional. Religious priests, brothers, and sisters often play a prominent role both in progressive organizations and in the articulation of progressive thought. Most religious orders have a social justice committee where their members can reflect on issues of faith and justice. Many orders support one or more congregationally based social justice projects. A number of orders have made structural decisions which reflect a progressive orientation. In a few cases, the commitment to justice has become a defining characteristic of religious orders.

This commitment on the part of religious orders is vital for Christian social activists, especially as it often provides an institutional base for their activities within the Church. This commitment is also significant for secular social movements who can count on the support of religious orders.[5] The Comité de priorités dans les dons of the Québec section of the Canadian Religious Conference gives $2.5 million annually to grassroots groups dedicated to social change – women's groups, tenants rights organizations, welfare rights groups, literacy groups, popular education groups, etc. This, moreover, is the tip of the iceberg, as religious orders also provide financial and other forms of support (for instance, office space) through a variety of channels. In a political context where government financing is increasingly tied to the meeting of program goals, the "fewer strings" attached to this support provides a critical margin of freedom.

The impact of the Catholic left upon the institutional Church can also be noted in the documents produced by the Assemblée des évêques du Québec.[6] In their annual May Day messages, the social affairs committee regularly addresses questions of poverty, social programs, working conditions, and economic structures. The bishops have offered support to social movements; for example, the endorsement of the 1995 Bread and Roses March organized by the women's movement.[7] So too, have they initiated alliances with social movements, as when they brought the unions, business, the cooperative movement, popular organizations, and the women's movement together around the statement Sortons le Québec de l'appauvrissement.[8] The bishops' theological committee has provided the justification for such Church involvement, arguing that solidarity with the poor is the basis for a faithful incarnation of the Christian faith in the contemporary world.[9]

Notwithstanding these public positions, important tensions remain. While each diocese has structures for addressing questions of faith and justice, many progressive Catholics feel that their concerns remain peripheral to the Church's concerns. In most diocesan planning, the allocation of financial and human resources does not reflect the bishops' teaching on the centrality of the justice struggle to Christian faith. At the parish level, the social teaching of the Church remains largely invisible and justice concerns are rapidly subsumed by a more traditional charity approach. Progressive Catholics thus continue to perceive their loose network of organizations and informal groups as the primary site of a Christian commitment to social change.

CHRISTIANS WORKING FOR JUSTICE

I have chosen to examine two organizations among the various groups which form the Catholic left in Quebec. The first is the Québec City-based Carrefour de pastorale en monde ouvrier, commonly called CAPMO. The second is the Jesuit Faith and Justice Centre in Montreal, the Centre justice et foi. This examination draws primarily upon internal documents from these two organizations. My hope is that it will allow the reader to discover aspects of the Catholic left in Quebec that a general discussion might not.

The Carrefour de pastorale en monde ouvrier was founded in the mid-seventies as a meeting place for pastoral workers involved in working-class ministry.[10] Its original members were staff persons of the working-class Catholic Action movements, the Jeunesse ouvrière chrétienne, and the Mouvement des travailleurs chrétiens, parish priests in working-class neighbourhoods, worker priests and women religious, lay activists and religious involved in various forms of neighbourhood action. Its purpose was to bring the Church closer to working-class reality, to promote working-class ministry, and to provide support for those involved in ministry among the working-class. While the membership is no longer restricted to pastoral workers and the organized working-class is no longer seen as the paradigmatic social movement, overall, the group has retained its original character.

At the centre of CAPMO's functioning is a monthly supper and thematic discussion which brings together 15 to 30 activists. The minutes of this meeting are then circulated to a large network of about 200 people. The group defines its orientation in terms of four axes: working-class and popular reality; a "projet de société" or alternative social vision; international solidarity; and spirituality for social activists. Again, these priorities have been present from the beginning of the organization, although there has been a shift in emphasis. In the seventies and early eighties, workplace struggles were the main focus of the group's discussions, taking up half the meetings. However, the unemployment crisis and the growing deterioration of popular neighbourhoods has led to an increasing interest in non-workplace subjects, and discussion of the need for an alternative social project has become increasingly central to the group's work.[11]

Founded in 1983, the Centre justice et foi is the social justice centre of the French Canada province of the Society of Jesus. Its work is divided among three sectors. The programs sector organizes various public activities and study sessions. This sector's responsibilities include the Soirées relations, a series of monthly public meetings on social issues in Montréal and Québec City which draw 75 to 100 participants. A second sector works exclusively on the question of immigration and cultural pluralism. Four times a year, this sector publishes a bulletin called *Vivre ensemble*. Finally, the Centre justice et foi incorporated the monthly current affairs journal *Rélations*, founded in 1941.

The Centre justice et foi describes itself as a centre for social analysis. Neither a political action group concerned with organizing the public nor a lobby group, it provides a variety of forums in which social activists, professionals, academics, and other intellectuals committed to social change can reflect upon social and political issues. The objective is not only to develop an ongoing analysis of Québec society but to generate concrete alternatives. Its priorities are similar to those of CAPMO: a "projet de société" or alternative social vision, international solidarity, new ethical questions, the status of women in Church and society, and Christianity in the context of modernity.

Important structural differences distinguish these two organizations. CAPMO is a relatively small organization with a budget of less than $50,000 and between one and three part-time staff persons, each of whom works a twenty-five-hour week for movement wages. With a paid staff of between ten and fifteen persons, including a librarian and four support staff, the Centre justice et foi is a much larger organization. As the apostolate of a prestigious men's religious order which provides most of its funding, it is financially more stable than CAPMO, which has no recurrent funding and is dependent upon various grants and membership fees.

CAPMO's structure is that of a popular organization; its members form a general assembly which determines the organization's priorities and elects a board of directors.[12] Staff are seen as members of the organization, whose salaries permit a greater participation, but it is expected that all the members will do a share of the work required by the organization. The Centre justice et foi has no membership and two-thirds of the appointed board are Jesuits. Its director and the editor of the magazine are both appointed by the Jesuit provincial. The task of running the Centre, including the determination of its priorities, falls largely on the professional staff.

A RADICALIZATION OF CHRISTIAN BELIEF AND PRACTICE

The Christian left in Quebec came into being in the turmoil that followed the Quiet Revolution and Vatican II. The so-called "crise de l'action catholique," born out of the adoption of a class-struggle framework by several Catholic Action movements, undoubtedly provided the kindling to light the fire. This *crise* signaled a breakdown in Catholic social teaching wherein Catholic social activists rejected the traditional third way philosophy[13] and challenged the Church hierarchy's authority in social and political matters. The institutional Church responded to this crisis by establishing the Commission on the Laity and the Church under the leadership of the sociologist and Catholic layman Fernand Dumont.[14] However, in spite of the heavy emphasis of the Dumont Commission on justice concerns in the modernization of the Church, the emergent Christian left was highly critical of its findings, which it perceived to be overly concerned with the renewal of Church structures and insufficiently attentive to the plight of the working class. For this reason, Jean-Paul Hétu, a staff person of the Central des syndicats nationaux who represented the Mouvement des travailleurs chrétiens on the commission, refused to sign the final report.

CAPMO was born in these heady days of the seventies. Moreover, in Québec City, the bitter labour conflict was fought at the Pavillion St-Dominique, a senior citizens' home belonging to a women's religious order.[15] The religious order's refusal to negotiate a first contract with their employees, and their subsequent hiring of scab labour, underscored the distance between the Church's social teaching and its actions. Pastoral workers involved in working class ministry perceived a Church unable to take the side of "les petits travailleurs," reluctant to engage in social conflict and suspicious of organized labour. It is thus not surprising to find that relations between CAPMO and the diocesan Church have often been conflictual. One of the most dramatic moments was when Cardinal Roy, then president of the Pontifical Council for Justice and Faith, arriving in a limousine, crashed a study session and delivered a tongue lashing to the assembled members. The diocesan Church has consistently refused to provide financial support for CAPMO or to recognize its ministry. On the other hand, the organization remains jealously protective of its autonomy from Church structures. Yet, in spite of this conflictual history, the institutional Church has often called upon CAPMO expertise in social justice issues. Vivian Labrie, one of its current staff people sits on the social affairs committee of the Assemblée des évêques du Québec. Indeed, in 1997, CAPMO was the initiator and co-author of the bishops' annual May Day letter.

The political and theological turmoil of the seventies also affected *Relations,* where ideological conflict brought about the replacement of the editorial board. The Centre itself, however, came into existence in the more peaceful early eighties as the result of a decision by the Jesuits to consolidate their social apostolate. This decision itself reflects a move by Jesuits worldwide to create a social justice centre in each of their provinces. In spite of this greater institutional grounding, however, the orientation document of the Centre justice et foi clearly reflects the critical spirit of the Catholic left, insisting on the need to understand social issues from the point of view of the poor and the need to compensate for the Church's over-insistence on liturgical and sacramental practices. The same document defines the Centre's relationship to the hierarchical Church as one of "solidarity without subordination," a definition made easier by the unique position the Jesuits occupy in the Roman Catholic Church. The Centre's publications are widely read and quoted within Church circles, and the expertise of its staff is frequently called upon.

THE OPTION FOR THE POOR AND A COMMITMENT TO SOCIAL CHANGE

Since the late sixties, Latin American liberation theology has played a major role in the self-understanding of progressive Christians in Québec. This influence is almost exclusive, there being little or no awareness of liberation theologies in Africa or Asia. The only exception to this rule is American feminist theology, which is widely read by Quebec feminists, who are also responsible for much of its translation. The relationship with liberationist movements within the Latin American Church is thus a privileged one upon which progressive Catholics in Quebec have drawn for the renewal of their own reflection on Christian belief and practice. At critical moments, solidarity movements with Chile, Central America, and more recently with Chiapas, have profoundly shaped progressive Christian political reflection. Theological exchanges have provided new frameworks. One has only to think of Gustavo Guttierez's seminar at the Université de Montréal in the summer of 1968 or the Brazilian theologian Ivone Gebarra's ongoing dialogue with Quebec feminists. The contributions of returning missionaries, study tours in Latin America, and various workshops have provided the occasion to appropriate and adapt liberationist frameworks.

The theological self-understanding of both the Centre justice et foi and CAPMO reflect this liberationist perspective. Both insist that discipleship in Christ requires effective solidarity with the oppressed: that to work for justice is to continue the work of Christ's incarnation and that the encounter with the poor is a place to encounter God. But again the structural differences between the two organizations effect how they live out these insights. The Centre justice et foi insists upon a discrete witness to the Gospel through its work for justice. For CAPMO, the sharing of meals, prayer, and liturgical practices are integrated into the life of the group which forms what its members call "a community of activists." Moreover, its commitment to developing a spirituality for activists leads the group as a worshipping community to innovate in this domain.

Politically, the evolution of the Christian left has mirrored that of progressive social forces more generally. Thus its radicalization of the seventies and the insistence on class analysis echoed debates within unions and political parties, popular rights organizations and international solidarity groups.[16] We find at that time in the Christian left discussion and arguments over Marxism and social democracy, vanguardism and *ouvrièrisme*, nationalism and internationalism. So too, the crisis of the left in the 1980s had severe repercussions for the Christian left. Some groups disappeared, others lost membership. All suffered from the collective demobilization after the referendum defeat of 1980 and the disintegration of the coalition between the Parti québécois and various social movements.[17] At the same time, both the secular and Christian left witnessed the emergence of new social forces, especially the women's movement. In the 1990s, the struggle against the neoliberal agenda and the search for an alternative mobilized the energies of progressive forces, both Christian and secular.

This tight relationship between the politics of the Christian left and those of the secular left is not surprising. Rather, it reflects the Christian left's understanding of itself not as an alternative to the secular left, but as part and parcel of progressive social movements. This self-understanding represents the full rejection of pre-Vatican II triumphalism and the Catholic vanguardism which dominated Catholic Action movements before the 1960s. The concern of the Christian left is not to build a Christian society but to build, alongside others, a society of justice.

The political evolution of the left is clearly visible in the work of both CAPMO and the Centre justice et foi. Both organizations work on a large range of issues, are involved in a diversity of debates, struggles, and coalitions, and maintain a large number of political and social alliances.

For CAPMO, the eighties were marked by concern with plant closures, the abatement of workplace conflicts, the Jeunesse ouvrière chrétienne's campaign around youth unemployment and poverty, the disappearance of worker priests and religious, and the weakening of links with unions. These events reshaped its political agenda. Increasingly, the word *populaire* replaced *ouvrier.* Job creation, the revitalization of Quebec City's downtown core, fiscal equity, and the struggle against social and economic exclusion became central preoccupations. In the nineties, in the wake of the Canada-U.S. Free Trade Agreement, the organization and its membership actively participated in the creation of a coalition of union and community organizations, Solidarité populaire Québec, and played an important role in the elaboration of that coalition's *Charte d'un Québec populaire.* Similarly, in response to the continuing deterioration of the central neighbourhoods of Québec City, they joined in creating a community development coalition, the Carrefour de relance de l'économie et de l'emploi du centre de Québec.

Thus, in the context of the latest round of welfare reform and budget cutting, it is not surprising to see CAPMO highlight the social project beyond the reform, initiating the Zero Poverty Clause which was defended by community organizations at the fall 1996 Economic Summit. In the autumn of 1997, they also proposed the extra-parliamentary White Paper on the Elimination of Poverty which has gathered a wide base of support.[18]

Since its beginnings, the Centre justice et foi has dealt with a broader range of issues. In the nineties, these included economic issues such as the hegemony of neoliberal economic doctrine, the dismantling of the welfare state, the impact of new technologies, and the reorganization of work. Yet they also include questions such as the place of native peoples in Quebec society, the urgent need for a civic nationalism, the construction of a shared public culture, the deconfessionalization of the school system (which the Centre supports), and Canadian refugee policy. In spite of its important contributions to the national debate, its relationship with a local context shapes CAPMO's political focus. The Centre's agenda is largely determined by its national mandate. Thus, for instance, in its work on "un Québec cassé en deux," the economic and social polarization of Quebec society is understood not only in terms of economic polarization but also the social disintegration of peripheral regions.[19] Thus the Centre examined not only the economic and social deterioration of Montréal but also the impact of the concentration of government services on regional development.

As a general rule, the primary emphasis in the work of CAPMO remains animation and mobilization, while the Centre justice et foi emphasizes analysis and conscientisation. At the same time, CAPMO's work focuses more sharply on social activists and on the empowerment of the poor as "knowers." The Centre serves a broader public and seeks to harness the credibility of knowledge for the service of the poor. The more limited resources of CAPMO forces it to rely upon imaginative and innovative methods, while the Centre's greater resources allow it to provide regular forums for discussion and reflection as well as publish high quality materials. CAPMO's work is more project-driven, its priorities more tightly linked to evolving social dynamics and the interests of its membership. The Centre's work is more production-driven, built around its publications and organizational commitments.

CONCLUSION

A diversity of voices and opinions exist within the loose network of organizations, groups, and individuals which make up the Catholic left in Quebec. The analysis of Carrefour de pastorale en monde ouvrier and the Centre justice et foi highlights this network's shared option for the economically impoverished, the socially marginalized, and the politically excluded and its commitment to making this option matter both politically and theologically.

Over the last three decades the Christian left has expanded its political vision. It no longer defines oppression and unjust social structures strictly in terms of class analysis. Yet it continues to understand social and economic realities to be conditioned by an unequal balance of power. Furthermore, progressive Christians have rejected a stance of political neutrality. The existence of social and political conflict requires taking sides. For progressive Quebec Christians, the option for the poor is not an abstract decision. Rather it requires concrete social engagement among and alongside the poor and an effective solidarity with social movements committed to change. Finally, the Catholic left accepts the magisterium, or teaching authority, of the poor. Emphasizing the poor as social actors and their role as agents of social change holds them up as "knowers" whose position in society allows them to have an authoritative vision. The Christian left are thus less interested in being the "voice of the voiceless" than in empowering the silenced to speak and be heard. CAPMO and the Centre justice et foi, each in its own way, embody this fundamental option of Quebec's Catholic left.

NOTES

1 Gregory Baum, *The Social Imperative* (New York: Paulist Press, 1979):92–6. See also his *The Catholic Church in Québec* (Ottawa: Novalis, 1991); and "The Catholic Left in Québec," in *Culture and Social Change*, ed. Colin Leys and Marguerite Mendell (Montréal: Black Rose, 1992):140–54.

2 See also Paul Reny et Jean-Paul Rouleau, "Charismatiques et sociopolitiques dans l'Église catholique au Québec," *Social Compass* 25 (1978):125–43; Jean-Guy Vaillancourt "Les groupes sociopolitiques dans le catholicisme québécois contemporain," in *Les mouvements religieux aujourd'hui. Théories et pratiques*, ed. J.-P. Rouleau et J. Zylberberg (Montreal: Bellarmin, 1984):261–82.

3 Gregory Baum, "The Catholic Left in Quebec," 151.

4 Jean Richard et Louis O'Neill, eds., *La question sociale hier et aujourd'hui. Colloque ducentenaire de Rerum novarum* (Quebec: Presses de l'Université Laval, 1993); Michel Beaudin et Guy Paiement, eds., *Sans emploi, peut-on vivre?* (Montreal: Fides, 1994); Michel Beaudin et al., *Le pouvoir de l'argent et le développement solidaire* (Montreal: Fides, 1997); Michel Beaudin et al., *Intervenir à contre-courant: de nouvelles pratiques solidaires* (Montreal, Fides,1998).

5 For a discussion of the future of religious orders' relationship with community organizations, see Jean Robitaille, "Jacques Belanger et l'héritage des communautés religieuses: Y aura-t-il une vie après la mort?" *Vie ouvrière* 1996 (mars-avril):12–17.

6 See Gérard Rocher, ed., *La justice sociale comme bonne nouvelle. Messages sociaux, économiques et politiques des évêques du Québec, 1972–1984*. (Montreal: Bellarmin, 1983). Most subsequent major statements are available through Fides, Saint-Laurent, Quebec.

7 Comité des affaires sociales de l'Assemblée des évêques du Québec, Pour en finir avec la pauvreté des femmes, mai 1995. Organized by the Fédération des femmes du Québec, the Marche du pains et des roses addressed issues of poverty and violence. Women walked throughout Québec for ten days, converging on Québec City for a final

demonstration in which 20,000 people participated. Religious communities and local parishes expressed their support in various ways, including lodging and ringing Church bells to mark the march's passage.

8 Claude Béland et al., *Sortons le Québec de l'appauvrissement* (Montréal: Assemblée des évêques du Québec, 1994).

9 Comité de théologie de l'Assemblée des évêques du Québec, *L'engagement des communautés chrétiennes dans la société* (Saint-Laurent: Fides, 1994).

10 Carrefour des agents de pastorale en monde ouvrier, *Manifeste pour une pastorale ouvrière* (1980).

11 See Vivian Labrie, "Faisons-le et ça se fera," in Kevin Arsenault et al., *Une soupe au caillou. Réflexions sur l'injustice économique* (Montréal: Paulines, 1997):49–80.

12 For a discussion of democratic structures and functioning as a hallmark of a popular organizations, see *Échos du comité aviseur de l'action communautaire autonome*, 1999 (automne).

13 The third way posited that Roman Catholic social teaching offered an alternative to both capitalism and socialism, based on interclass friendship and cooperation. This philosophy explains why the Confédération des travailleurs catholiques du Canada (CTCC), forerunner to the Confédération des syndicats nationaux (CSN), did not maintain strike funds, which they saw as counter to the quest for social harmony. One of the most important critiques of the third way remains Marie-Dominique Chenu, *La "doctrine sociale" de l'Église comme idéologie* (Paris: Éditions du Cerf, 1979).

14 Commission d'études sur des laïcs et l'Église, *L'Église du Québec, un héritage, un projet* (Montreal: Fides, 1972).

15 The magazine *Dossier "vie ouvrière"* dedicated two issues to the conflict: *Le Conflit du Pavillon St-Dominique*, 1974 (novembre); and *Quand l'employeur est l'Église*, 1974 (décembre).

16 See Yves Vaillancourt et al., *La conjoncture au Québec au début des années 1980* (Rimouski: La libraire socialiste de l'Est du Québec, 1980). See also Gregory Baum, "Politisés chrétiens: A Christian Marxist Network in Québec, 1974–1982," *Studies in Political Economy* 32 (Summer 1990):7–28.

17 Cf. Vincent Lemieux, "Partis politiques et vie politique" in Gérald Daigle (sous la direction de), *Le Québec en jeu* (Montreal: Presses de l'Université de Montréal, 1992):634–7.

18 See Vivian Labrie, "Choisir la citoyenneté," *Rélations*, 1997 (mai):103–7. Carrefour de pastorale en monde ouvrier, "Projet de loi sur l'élimination de la pauvreté," *Rélations*, 1997 (décembre):303–6. Under the leadership of the *Collectif pour une loi sur l'élimination de la pauvreté*, this proposal has received the support of a wide spectrum of Québec society.

Its primary focus is on a legislated commitment to the elimination of poverty, the social and economic protection of the poorest fifth of the population, and the involvement of this sector of the population in conceiving and implementing anti-poverty measures. More than 1500 organizations, including unions, youth groups, religious communities, women's groups, school boards and councils, and social service agencies, have officially endorsed the project. The supporting petition presented to the National Assembly gathered the signatures of 215,000 individuals, resulting in the adoption of the law in the spring of 2002. While groups are critical of the law in its adopted form, it is the result of this mobilization and pressure put on the government.

19 See Julien Harvey et al., "Un Québec cassé en deux," *Rélations*, 1988 (novembre):263–76; and Guy Paiement et al., "Le Québec cassé en deux 2: Le pouvoir caché," *Rélations*, 1990 (avril):71–86.

5 Religion, Emancipation, and Human Rights

GREGORY BAUM

The presentations of my colleagues have concentrated on the humanistic dimension of the religious heritage. Ursula Franklin saw in religion a counter-force to mechanistic thinking, Arvind Sharma found in the world religions support for human rights, Denis Goulet spoke of religion as a resource for life-sustaining development, and Carolyn Sharp presented religion as a spiritual force for emancipatory practice. Liberating religion does exist.

COMMITMENT TO JUSTICE AND RECONCILIATION

In the context of this volume it may not be out of place to tell the story of my own religious commitment to justice and reconciliation. My first major interest in theology was the ecumenical movement of the 1950s, which fostered mutual understanding between Catholics and Protestants, overcoming inherited prejudices, and striving for ultimate reconciliation. What I learned in that movement was the transformative power of dialogue. By listening to others with a sympathetic ear, we come to see them in a new light, become aware of our own prejudices, and discover new insights that allow us to reread our own religious tradition in a creative way. Dialogue is more than conversation. Dialogue transforms both partners, making them more open to one another and more faithful to their own religious inheritance.

My experience in the 1950s convinced me that dialogue is a powerful intellectual exercise capable of being practised in our encounter with "others," heirs of traditions that seem foreign or strange to us. I learned much later that dialogue can also be instrumentalized by the powerful, used as a tool to keep oppressed or disadvantaged people smiling, diffuse their anger, and reconcile them with the status quo. That this abuse is possible, however, in no way weakens the transformative function of authentic dialogue.

Because I had written my doctoral dissertation on an ecumenical topic, Pope John XXIII in 1960 appointed me to become a theological advisor at the Secretariat of Christian Unity, which was one of the ecclesiastical commissions instituted to prepare and accompany Vatican Council II (1962–65). This was a great honour for a young theologian. It was a privilege to participate in the events that changed the teaching and practice of the Catholic Church in significant ways. The new approach was the result of a struggle at the Council. The most controversial documents were prepared by the Secretariat of Christian Unity, then under the direction of Cardinal Bea. While official Catholic teaching had condemned the ecumenical movement in the past, the conciliar document prepared by the Secretariat and approved by the Council now praised the ecumenical movement as an initiative of the Spirit in the churches.[1]

Pope John XXIII also asked the secretariat to prepare a statement on the Church's relation to the Jewish people to correct the anti-Jewish current in Christian teaching and promote friendship and cooperation between Christians and Jews. Since I had just written a small book on this topic *The Jews and the Gospel* (New York: Newman Press, 1961), and inspired by my commitment to justice and reconciliation, I was appointed to the committee that was to produce this text. The issue was important to me also for personal reasons: while I had a Christian upbringing, my parents' background was in fact Jewish. In the past, the Church had taught that the Jews, by not believing in Christ, had forfeited the ancient covenant, were now deprived of divine grace, and could find salvation only by becoming Christians. To overcome the deadly cultural consequences of this teaching and in reliance on a strong New Testament passage,[2] the Vatican Council affirmed that despite the refusal of the Jews to believe in Jesus, God's covenant with them remains intact, they continue to be God's first-loved people, and for this reason, have no need to turn to the Christian faith.[3]

The Vatican Council also retrieved the ancient Christian teaching that God's Spirit, summoning people to goodness and truth, was operative in the whole of human history. The divine Spirit revealed in Christ also communicates itself through secular wisdom and the practice of the world religions. This new perspective enabled the Church to redefine its mission in terms of dialogue and cooperation in the service of peace, justice, and reconciliation.[4] While the Church in the nineteenth century had rejected religious freedom and civil liberties in general, the Vatican Council now affirmed freedom of religion and the respect for human rights.[5]

These were very exciting times. Because the Council also retained some of the more traditional texts, a lively debate ensued over the degree to which the Church should open itself to the new perspective, a debate in which I took an active part. In books, articles, and public lectures, I defended the most open interpretation of the conciliar teaching.

Then, in the early seventies, I was converted to a new outlook and became an intellectual of the left. Under the impact of Latin American liberation theology I realized that in my thinking I had followed the Catholic trust in the organic nature of society and the liberal trust in goodwill, overlooking the conflictive nature of society: the class struggle on the national and international level carried on by the economic and political élites against the lower sector of the population. A strong influence on me was my friendship with a brilliant American woman, Rosemary Radford Ruether, a theologian, socialist, and feminist, who was to become one of the most original and productive religious thinker in North America. Since that time I have thought of myself as a member of the Catholic left, a worldwide network within the Catholic Church that regards commitment to justice and liberation as an essential dimension of the Christian faith. I am actually able to document my theological development from the pages of a small review, *The Ecumenist*, which I have edited for over thirty years.

While the Catholic left or, more inclusively, the Christian left is a minority movement within the churches, it did have great influence on their official teaching. The emancipatory understanding of faith, hope, and charity has been acknowledged in the public statements of Catholic and Protestant ecclesiastical institutions. It is in keeping with traditional dogma to see God as the just and merciful transcendent power who releases in people's hearts the capacity to struggle for a just, kind, and responsible society respectful of the earth. In conditions of grave inequality, the love of which the Bible speaks transforms itself into a yearning for justice and an impulse to act so that the heavy burdens be lifted from the shoulders of the poor and oppressed. The divine presence reveals itself on earth in social manifestations of love, justice, and peace.

Moving to Montreal in 1986 was a great pleasure for me, in part because a significant Catholic left still exists in Quebec with its centres, reviews, and regular meetings, often collaborating in projects with the groups and organizations of the secular left. Moving to Montreal also led me to the Karl Polanyi Institute where I was introduced to *The*

Great Transformation, took part in lively discussions on political economy, and became a friend of Margie Mendell. I was greatly impressed by Karl Polanyi's critique of the self-regulating market system which paid serious attention to ethical and cultural issues. If Latin American liberation theologians had been acquainted with his thought, they would have found a more reflective distance from Marxism and discovered concepts allowing them to take seriously ethical and cultural factors.

THE AMBIGUITY OF RELIGION

In the early seventies I studied sociology at the New School in New York City. As a Christian believer I wanted to listen to the religious criticism produced by thinkers of the Enlightenment. Marx was not altogether wrong when he said that religion was the opium of the people, nor was Nietzsche altogether wrong when he saw religion as an expression of resentment felt by the weak and fearful against the bold and creative, nor was Freud altogether wrong when he said that religion was people's pathological refusal to grow up and face reality. Yet more careful social scientific research has showed that these negative evaluations of religion are not the whole truth, that the positive and negative exist in religion side by side, and thus that the world religions are ambivalent historical phenomena.

Following Freud's psychoanalytical approach, Erich Fromm came to distinguish in religion "authoritarian" and "humanistic trends."[6] While for some believers God is the power that controls their lives from above, for others God is the grace that empowers them to assume responsibility for themselves. Following Marx's critical sociological approach, Karl Mannheim came to distinguish in culture and religion "ideological" and "utopian" trends. In his book, *Ideology and Utopia*, he provided categories for examining the weight and power of ideas and symbols in history.[7] He defined "ideology" as the cultural trends that legitimate the existing order, make its failures invisible, and stabilize the ruling powers; and he named "utopia" the cultural trends that reveal the injustices of the existing order, imagine the coming of an alternative society, and create restlessness and desire for social change. Mannheim recognized religion as an ambiguous, pluriform force in history.

Learning from the writings of the non-orthodox Marxist, Ernst Bloch,[8] Karl Mannheim came to acknowledge the social power of the utopian imagination. In his book, he arrived at the conclusion that the emancipatory movements in Western society, including the Marxist movement, were guided by utopian images that were ultimately derived from the messianic promises recorded in the Bible. Suffering alone does not explain the yearning for an alternative society; what is equally necessary is the conviction that the present order is at odds with the nature of things, that its power is temporary, and that the promises of a higher destiny are written into history.

Mannheim was equally sensitive to the overt and hidden ideological uses of religion. Ideological religion is still thriving. Allow me to give two examples that are not well known, where men in powerful positions think that religious practices can help their cause. The first example is amusing, the second serious.

One of East Germany's leading Communist ideologues, Jürgen Kuczynski, made the following statement on the value of prayer at the 1987 Writer's Congress in the German Democratic Republic:

> Despite the annoyances of every day and the troubling things that happen, Christians are reminded in their morning and evening prayer that human history in its totality, including cosmos, heaven and paradise, is ultimately a wonderful thing. In Islam, believers are reminded of this three times a day. For some time now I have searched for a substitute for this kind of prayer, reminding us that, despite the daily troubles and the obstacles we so often encounter, our socialism is a wonderful thing: no unemployment, no homelessness ... the list is long. I have tried to write an article on a socialist prayer-substitute, but I did not have to wait for its rejection by the authorities: it had already been rejected by my friends. But you, authors that you are, you may have an idea of what we can do to remind ourselves once or twice each day of the wonderful thing that inspires us – so that we recognize that the daily decisions, while important and having an impact on our lives, are nonetheless secondary: the wonderful thing prevails.[9]

A different kind of utilitarian interest in religion has recently been taken by the World Bank. Recognizing that the structural adjustment policies imposed upon the so-called developing countries increases public misery and destabilizes society, the World Bank has become concerned with "world governance," that is, the ensemble of factors that protect good order and assure social stability under the difficult conditions created by the globalization of the economy. Among these factors, religion holds a special place. The World Bank started a dialogue with religious thinkers in the 1995 Conference on Ethics and Spiritual Values held in Washington D.C., followed by the 1998 Conference on World Faith and Development held at Lambeth Palace in London, at which the leaders of the world religions participated.[10] Over the last decade, religious leaders all over the world have denounced the globalization of the unregulated market system and claimed that the neoliberal policies undermine the regional traditions of solidarity. Will the dialogue initiated by the World Bank make religious leaders look more kindly upon the World Bank's economic policies? Will the World Bank offer these leaders financial assistance to gain their confidence?

PROPHETIC RELIGION

When theologians studied the writings of Ernst Bloch and Karl Mannheim, they were amazed by the affinity between the social scientific concepts of "critique" and "utopia" and the religious categories of classical Hebrew prophecy. The Hebrew prophets, preaching in the kingdoms of Israel and Judah of the eighth and seventh centuries BCE, were appalled by the social injustices in their society in violation of the Torah given to Israel by God. The prophets preached God's severe judgment on oppression and exploitation and God's special love for the poor and the weak. The prophets introduced the people to critical thinking in regard to their own social existence and called for the conversion of hearts and an alternative practice. At the same time, the prophets also sustained the people in hope, proclaiming that the divine promises had not been withdrawn from them. God would act in their midst to transform them and make them into a faithful people that loved truth and justice. The prophets had their own religious language for what today's social scientists call "critique" and "utopia."

In ordinary speech people are called prophets when they predict the future. Yet in the language of the Bible and the theological tradition, the prophet is one who announces God's will as both judgment on injustice and promise of rescue. Jesus stood in this prophetic tradition. Max Weber draws upon the biblical vocabulary when he distinguishes between priestly and prophetic religion, where the former sustains and blesses the believing community while the latter judges it and calls its members to a conversion of heart. In the history of the Christian churches, priestly religion has predominated.

The historical episodes of prophetic religion have, perhaps not surprisingly, fascinated left-leaning social and political scientists, from Friedrich Engels to Michael Walzer. Engels was puzzled by the last book of the New Testament, the Apocalypse, which cursed the Roman Empire as the Whore of Babylon and by Thomas Muenzer, whose preaching supported the Peasant Revolt of 1525.[11] At the end of the list of the fascinated stands Michael Walzer, who has produced studies of the Puritan revolution in seventeenth-century England and the biblical Exodus story as influences on western revolutionary movements.[12]

Why are religions capable of such diverse interpretations? Why can the same religion, such as Christianity, give rise to such divergent courses of action? The answer to this is that religions constitute hermeneutic communities: they reread their sacred texts in new historical circumstances and hear a new message addressing the problems with which they are wrestling. The creative reading of the sacred texts also explains why religions are auto-regenerative traditions. Cultures come and go, languages are created and die, but religion survives the breakdown of civilization. The explanation for this resiliance is that religions are communicated by symbols, gestures, and words, all of which are capable of being reread and thus of bringing forth unexpected meanings in new historical situations. Ancient religions can utter new messages – messages of oppression or liberation.

The contemporary return of religion to the public sphere dramatically reveals the ambiguous character of religion. While we observe fundamentalist movements in all the world religions, with their opposition to cultural pluralism and humanistic values, we also observe in the same religions the spread of social movements promoting justice, freedom, and peace. In recent decades, emancipatory religion has had its martyrs such as Archbishop Oscar Romero, assassinated because of his solidarity with the poor in El Salvador, and Bishop Juan Gerardi Conedera, assassinated as chair of the human rights commission of Guatemala. Over the last few years, let me add, the major Canadian churches denounced as immoral the turn to neoliberal economic policies and supported the Canadian Jubilee Initiative as part of an international Christian movement in support of debt relief for the poor countries of the South in the year 2000.[13]

In the past, prophetic religion has revealed itself in relatively brief historical episodes. The message of the Hebrew prophets and the prophetic ministry of Jesus were not allowed to play a major role in the history of the Christian churches. For the sake of institutional stability, the churches have on the whole preferred conformity to the political and economic system of their society. That a major theological movement of universal outreach makes "the prophetic principle" the principal hermeneutical key for interpreting the Christian message is, I think, a twentieth- and twenty-first century phenomenon.

According to this theology, often called "political theology," fidelity to the biblical revelation means the willingness to look at one's culture and society in the light of God's demand for justice and mercy. Culture and society are here seen as standing under God's judgment condemning oppression, exploitation, and all other forms of injustice. Biblical faith summons forth a critical look at one's own world, and biblical hope and love summons forth transformative action.

Political theology offers a socially relevant interpretation of the Christian doctrine of original sin. Humanity is here seen as wounded by the institutions of its own making. Because of a desire to dominate and a love of possessions, human beings create structures that, even while fulfilling many beneficial functions, retain oppressive features damaging to body and soul. The greatest human achievements remain imperfect and flawed. Life on earth cannot fully escape this ambiguity.

Political theology also offers a socially relevant interpretation of divine grace. God is here seen as redeemer or rescuer, operative in people's hearts, taming their self-seeking and generating altruism. God is here believed to empower people to wrestle for a more just society and in doing so to become themselves transformed into more just and loving persons. Yet even the highest accomplishments, achieved with God's help, retain a dark side that must be confronted.

CRITICAL THEORY

It is not a coincidence, in my opinion, that one of the important thinkers who built his theology around "the prophetic principle," the Protestant theologian Paul Tillich, was closely associated with the Marxist philosophers of the Frankfurt School. In the 1920s, Tillich, then a professor at the University of Frankfurt, guided Theodor Adorno in his doctoral dissertation and helped Max Horkheimer to obtain a professorship at the university.[14] The critical theorists of the Frankfurt School were keenly aware of the dark side of all human accomplishments and developed a critical approach intended to disclose the dehumanizing implications of well-intentioned political and cultural achievements. All thought, they argued, must begin with negation. What must have attracted Tillich to these critical theorists was also their suspicion of objectivity in the human sciences. Humans can discover the truth about the reality to which they belong, these theorists held, only if their research is guided by an emancipatory commitment. The study of society that sees itself as objective, inevitably reinforces the oppressive and alienating features implicit in the social reality. These critical reflections led the Frankfurt philosophers to a dynamic understanding of the interdependence between theory and practice.

What was the inspiration of the Frankfurt School's call for negation and commitment? To point to Marxism is not sufficient, since the starting point of critical theory was the accusation that Marxism did not engage in systematic self-criticism of its ideas and practices, and that its political failures were to a large extent due to this complacency. Marxists regarded their movement as free of ambiguity: the party, they thought, had no dark side that deserved careful analysis. Despite their critique of Marxism, the Frankfurt School theorists regarded themselves as Marxists of sorts, just as Tillich at that time considered himself a Marxist of sorts.

What then was the inspiration of the Frankfurt School's call for negation and commitment? Several commentators have argued that the founders of the Frankfurt School were Jewish and that, even though completely secular, they were heirs of the Bible's unconditional demand for social justice. They translated the prophetic tradition into secular discourse. Whether or not this is so, it is not surprising that theologians who attach central importance to the prophetic principle and see their theology as sustaining the human struggle for liberation have recognized an affinity with the Frankfurt School and apply its critical theory in their own theological reflections.[15]

Let me focus on an element of critical theory that provides an insight to keep in mind in the defense of human rights. The Frankfurt School, as I mentioned above, had a keen sense of the dark side of culture and society, including the progressive movements that in the name of truth and science sought to transform the social order. Even these movements could not escape the ambiguity of earthly existence. The Frankfurt critics therefore called for "the end of innocent critique." What did they mean by this? A critique of ideas or a system is deemed "innocent" if it is not self-reflective, that is, if it fails critically to explore the range of its own implications and its possible social consequences. The rejection of oppressive ideologies and structures remains "innocent" if 1) it does not rescue the grain of truth that may be contained in these ideologies or structures and 2) it does not ask itself what its social impact will be once it becomes a dominant opinion and assumes cultural power. The Frankfurt School thought that Marxism had offered an "innocent critique" of bourgeois society because it did not attempt to retrieve the civil liberties that were part of the bourgeois revolution and because it did not develop a self-reflective discourse that would prevent it from becoming an oppressive ideology.

The Frankfurt School used the same critical principle in arguing against the many voices which, in the twenties and thirties, repudiated the Enlightenment. These voices included conservatives who wanted to secure the ideals and values of premodern Europe, the existentialists who lamented the loss of authenticity and the reification of personal life in modern society, the nationalists who rejected the universal values of the Enlightenment in favour of national values rooted in tradition, and the German Nazis who repudiated human rights and the reign of reason by an appeal to instinctive forces of blood and soil and the victory of the strong over the weak. Today's postmodern authors are latecomers with their rejection of the Enlightenment. The Frankfurt School worried not only about the rise of fascism in Europe but also about the other critics who rejected the Enlightenment in disregard of its emancipatory achievements and its struggle for universal justice.

The Frankfurt critics regarded these unqualified critiques as "innocent": they did not search for the kernel of truth in the philosophy they rejected, nor did they reflect on what the absence of a common ethical ideal would mean for Europe and the world. German historicists at the beginning of the twentieth century had already advanced the idea of cultural and ethical pluralism: they discarded the universality of reason and concluded that since reason was unable to create order in the world, order would have to be imposed by the powerful.

To defend the Enlightenment the Frankfurt critics began with negation. They formulated their own critique of the Enlightenment. They argued that the predominance of instrumental reason in European society had made the Enlightenment today the cause of alienation and an obstacle to human liberation. With Max Weber they thought that the dominance of instrumental reason was moving society into an "iron cage." Since instrumental reason was silent about values and only perfected the means of action, powerful decision makers were able to program society and bureaucratically control it in accordance with their own purposes. Today's technocratic form of Enlightenment, the Frankfurt philosophers argued, would lead to totalitarianism.

At the same time, the Frankfurt critics protested against an "innocent," unqualified rejection of the Enlightenment. They recalled that the original Enlightenment thinkers who turned to "reason" as the organ of human emancipation recognized the twofold nature of rationality, including substantive reason, dealing with ends, and instrumental or scientific reason, dealing with means. Substantive reason, they thought, offers grounds for liberty, equality, and solidarity as the ends of society. Substantive reason laid the foundation for a universal social ethics. Yet, according to the Frankfurt critics, the increasing dominance of scientific, technological, and bureaucratic rationality shattered public confidence in substantive reason and by doing so transformed the Enlightenment into the great obstacle to human emancipation. Still, instead of rejecting the Enlightenment in an unqualified way, the present task – according to the Frankfurt critics – was to decentre instrumental reason and in innovative ways, recover substantive reason dealing with ends. In the terminology of the Frankfurt critics, the critique of the Enlightenment must not be naïve, but dialectical, involving negation and retrieval. Reason must transcend technocratic rationality and concern itself again with the well-being of humans and their environment.

HUMAN RIGHTS

The United Nations Universal Declaration of Human Rights in 1948 was a historic moment of ethical retrieval. It is important to be aware that some critical thinkers in non-Western cultures see this declaration as an imperialistic gesture imposing a set of Western values upon the world. There are also postmodern authors who argue that any affirmation of universal truths or universal values is implicitly totalitarian. It is possible, I suppose, to read the universal declaration in this manner. It is true that the human rights tradition, like any human achievement, has its dark side: it can be used in an ideological fashion to enhance the exercise of domination.

Let me give a few examples. By emphasizing personal rights or civil liberties (and bracketing the socio-economic rights also affirmed in the declaration), Western nations have claimed cultural superiority over non-Western cultures. A one-sided emphasis on civil liberties is also being used to undermine institutions based on social solidarity such as families, labour unions, and cultural communities. By putting exclusive emphasis on socio-economic rights, governments of communist countries have tried to legitimate their suppression of civil liberties. The collective human rights affirmed in subsequent covenants of the United Nations[16] have also been abused by dictatorial regimes to defend their curtailment of civil liberties. The protests against human rights by non-Western and postmodern thinkers oblige us to pay more critical attention to the human rights tradition. One must not forget that this tradition exists in three distinct families – personal, socio-economic, and collective rights – and hence is not a single normative system imposed uniformly upon all cultures. The threefold human rights tradition refers rather to a set of competing moral claims that must find a rationally argued balance appropriate to the conditions of each locality. Nations can use the human rights tradition to defend their culture and the institutions based on social solidarity. This is the first argument that the declaration of human rights is not an imperialistic imposition of a Western value upon non-Western cultures. The second argument is even stronger. The United Nations offered no philosophical arguments in support of the declaration of human rights. It was deeply felt outrage over the massive crimes against humanity committed during World War II that persuaded nations to stand behind and solemnly sign the universal declaration. They were dismayed by these evil deeds because they violated the basic ethical norms of their own cultural and religious traditions. Each of these traditions, not just Western Enlightenment thought, provided substantive reasoning in support of human dignity and in defense of human rights. Substantive reasoning may not be uniform, but there is good evidence that on many essentials it arrives at common conclusions.

This has been demonstrated by the experience of international organizations such as the World Conference on Religion and Peace and the World Parliament of Religions. In the Louvain Declaration (1974) of the World Conference of Religion and Peace, the representatives of the world religions regretfully admit that their own tradition has contributed to injustice and violent conflict in the world; at the same time, they acknowledge that the most genuine and authentic values of their religious tradition stand for justice and peace and the protection of the weakest members of society. These religious leaders call for the conversion of their co-religionists to their deepest roots. In the terminology of the Frankfurt School, these leaders call for the rereading of the religious traditions out of an emancipatory commitment. Each religion thus discovers that it provides reasons for affirming human rights. In the words of the Louvain Declaration: "We are resolved henceforth to serve humanity together, each in the way most in keeping with the convictions of its spiritual family and the local circumstances. Drawing upon the inexhaustible resources of our several spiritual heritages, we are experiencing together the truth expressed by one of the poets in our midst, 'I walk on thorns, but firmly, as among flowers.'"[17]

NOTES

1 Walter Abbot, ed. "Decree on Ecumenism," in *Documents of Vatican II* (New York: Herder and Herder, 1966):341–67.

2 Apostle Paul's Epistle to the Romans 11:1 and 29.

3 "Declaration on the Relationship of the Church to non-Christians Religions, chapter 4," in Abbot, *Documents*:663–7.

4 Pastoral Constitution on the Church in the Modern World," Ibid., 199–308.

5 Declaration on Religious Freedom," Ibid., 675–98.

6 Erich Fromm, *Psychoanalysis and Religion* (New York: Bantam Books, 1967).

7 Karl Mannheim, *Ideology and Utopia* (New York: Harcourt, Brace & World, 1952 [1928]).

8 Ernst Bloch, *Geist der Utopie* (Frankfurt: Suhrkamp, 1964 [1919]).

9 Quoted by Randy Bytwerk in the October 1998 Newsletter on Churches in Germany directed by John Conway (jconway@interchange.ubc.ca). Her reference is *X. Schriftstellerkongress der Deutschen Demokratischen Republik* (Köln: Pahl-Rugenstein, 1988):24.

10 Gregory Baum, "Reflections on the Activities of the World Bank," *Concilium* 1999 (April).

11 Friedrich Engels in Karl Marx and Friedrich Engels. *On Religion*, intro. Reinhold Niebuhr (New York: Schocken Books, 1964):97–118.

12 Michael Walzer, *The Revolution of the Saints: A Study in the Origins of Radical Politics*, Cambridge: Harvard University Press, 1965; and, *Exodus and Revolution.* New York: Basic Books, 1985.

13 For literature of the Canadian Ecumenical Jubilee Initiative consult <jubilee@devp.org>.

14 Martin Jay, *The Dialectical Imagination: A History of the Frankfurt School.* Boston: Little, Brown and Comp., 1973, 24–5.

15 Best-known among the left-leaning critical theologians are Johann Baptist Metz, Jürgen Moltmann, and Dorothee Soelle in Germany, and Robert McAfee Brown, Matthew Lamb, Rosemary Ruether, and Rudolph Siebert in the U.S.A.

16 The International Covenant of Civil and Political Rights and the International Covenant of Economic, Social and Cultural Rights, both signed at the United Nations in 1966. See *The Human Rights Reader*, Walter Laqueur, ed. (New York: New American Library, 1989):215–33.

17 The declarations of the World Conference on Religion and Peace can be found on its website <www.wcrp.org>.

POLITICAL ECONOMY AND DEMOCRACY

6 West Indian from East Europe. Kari Polanyi Levitt

LLOYD BEST

I am delighted to participate in this volume to honour Kari Polanyi Levitt. Kari hails from a distinguished, acclaimed line. Her intellectual pedigree is unmistakably Austro-Hungarian, and she was educated in England. It was in Canada that she led most of her professional life, and in the Caribbean that her heart found reason to stay engaged, productive, and lucid.

Kari's is perhaps a tale of the global village. Not the global village created by the migration of capital and the disembedding of trade and production from their own context of culture and society but the one restored to wholeness by the migration of human empathy and concern, forged by bonds of mutual affection and enduring commitment over many long seasons of candid encounter and equal exchange.

Few can match Kari's contribution to scholarly endeavour and intellectual enterprise all over the Caribbean. Few can equal her contribution to Canada-West Indies relations. Such an achievement entitles her to more than the honorary citizenship she's won in the Caribbean community by acclaim as much as by adoption. Many who do not know her origins mistake her for a patriot born. This piece will joyfully try to weigh reasons.

A WEST INDIAN FROM EAST EUROPE

The motto of my old school in Trinidad is *Certant omnes sed non omnibus palma*. Many are called, few chosen. I count myself lucky to have been elected to be perhaps the closest of all the local collaborators to that West Indian from East Europe who spent her most productive days compensating for the havoc so long wreaked by The Enterprise of the Indies, that venture in globalization which Christopher Columbus, when he opted to go East by West, may not have launched, but was certainly the first to have done so effectively, definitively, and brutally. Kari countered in more ways than one. She went West by East. She began in Budapest and Vienna. I am lucky to have come to know what that means, having been taught as undergraduate in one place by Peter Bauer and Nickie Kaldor, and as graduate in another place, by Paul Streeten and Tommy Balogh. My good fortune was to have acquired intensely personal as well as professional reasons for following the progress of that brilliant and aptly celebrated set from these signal capitals which includes the Polanyis: Michael, Karl, and Ilona of one generation, and now Kari among the successors.

The setting in which this future would play itself out over nearly four decades was already cast in the early years, in a status of repeated "betweenity," the essence of our condition in the Caribbean. This state was also doubtless a clue to the region's fateful attraction both to the professional, with her particular philosophical and epistemological predisposition, and to the person – the political person – with her clear, unambiguous, and constant alignment to the poor and the powerless, the disadvantaged and the dispossessed, whatever their incarnation.

Kari was a Hungarian girl born in Vienna, bred in an English boarding school. When she entered the London School of Economics, she again found herself straddling two worlds, the newer red brick of Harold Laski and the older Oxbridge of Joan Robinson and John Maynard Keynes, with Nickie Kaldor somehow bridging the two, at the time LSE moved to Cambridge during World War II. At school Kari had known John Grell of Trinidad, later to be Games Master at the Queen's Royal College when I was at that institution. But it was during the London years that she first met West Indians as a clan. A young Arthur Lewis lectured to her. Lloyd Braithwaite was in town then, later joined by Elsa Goveia, Forbes Burnham, Errol Barrow, Michael Manley, and I think, Michael Beaubrun. Kari next went to Toronto. At the height of the Joe McCarthy interrogations, she kept on editing not a New Left but a far left review, in the cause not only of better wages and conditions for workers but also of intellectual independence, personal autonomy, and free expression.

As so often happens, it was through accident that she first forged her definitive link with the Caribbean. In 1961 Kari's professor at Toronto, Burton Keirstead, recruited her for a mostly statistical mission that took her to Trinidad, Jamaica, and the Mona Campus of the

University of the West Indies. She came to know William Demas and Lloyd Best, and not long after, Alister McIntyre and George Beckford.

For more than three-and-a-half decades, Kari's involvement with us in the Caribbean has been literally uninterrupted. She's delivered inspired output in the form of teaching, research, theoretical speculation, and public debate, in every corner of that Ocean Sea – Jamaica, Puerto Rico, Cuba, the Dominican Republic, Guyana, Trinidad, Barbados, Grenada, and where else? She has pursued expert work as a consultant to governments at both ends of the archipelago. She has moreover organized numberless fellowships and studentships in North America for West Indians, thereby expanding horizons and advancing careers at many different levels.

Kari is eminently worthy of being honoured at the moment of her Jubilee celebrations. Her Golden Age may have passed but not to Gall and Wormwood. Rather the mutation is to ripe maturity and abiding wisdom. We from the Caribbean admire, respect, love, and revere her. We want her to know and to feel all of that in no uncertain way. For our part, we want to think and feel it, and we want to announce and declare it, loud and clear.

OUR COLLABORATION

I am happy to be able to discuss the professional collaboration between us. That collaboration provided opportunity to build relationships with two or three generations of scholars, as much outside the Caribbean as inside. We look back with pleasure to contacts with Stephen Hymer of the New School of Social Research in New York, Osvaldo Sunkel of CEPAL in Santiago, Chile, Celso Furtado of North East Brazil and at one time at the University of Paris, and Giovanni Arrighi of Northern Italy. Ours was no more than an enduring enquiry jointly undertaken, an effort at common investigation and speculation, sometimes wrongly said to have amounted a New World School or a Plantation School.

Kari and I did have a core of treasured collaborators, including a number who at first were graduate students. But the association was always felicitously flexible and based on thinking that converged only at certain points, even where Levitt and Best were concerned, though we two in particular shared a great deal in outlook, orientation, and method. What have we done? In all frankness, I would say that the main thing is that, by attempting to devise macro- and microeconomics specific to the Caribbean case, we managed to unlock a few more secrets to add to those which Sir Arthur Lewis, undoubtedly the dean of Caribbean economists, had unlocked before us, having taken us a very long way on the road to penetration and insight.

We first began to suspect the virtue of applying orthodox theory to the Caribbean economy when we developed serious doubts over the industrial strategies governments were pursuing with far more zeal than success. Policy had clearly been inspired by lucid and pointed proposals published in the *Caribbean Review* in 1949 and 1950 by Dr Arthur Lewis, Principal of the UWI, as we entered the 1960s; proposals at the same time promoted, from his strategic position as Director of Research in the Anglo-American Caribbean Commission, by Dr Eric Williams, later Prime Minister (Premier) of Trinidad and Tobago from 1956 on. That is where we started in the middle 1960s in a highly charged atmosphere.

Pieces reflecting our early concerns go back to notes Kari and I exchanged during the course of the year 1962–63 that I spent in Georgetown as one of two UN Technical Assistance Board advisors to Dr Jagan's Economic Planning Division. Morsels that betray our group's early thinking have appeared in the *New World Quarterly*, mostly under the rubric of Edwin Carrington, now Secretary General of CARICOM, then a student, first at the UWI campus at Mona, later with Kari here at McGill. The *New World Quarterly* was a journal of Caribbean affairs we'd founded in Georgetown, Guyana, in 1963 and moved to UWI, Jamaica, in 1965. It was to be a vehicle for young faculty members and a rallying point mostly for UWI graduates attracted to these and related ideas who had returned to different corners of the region or engaged in post-graduate studies in North American universities.

Together Kari and I undertook a study that would fathom the workings of the Caribbean economy and if possible explain why it experienced bouts of rapid expansion and great prosperity punctuated by long periods of stagnation or contraction. Our base material was the economic history of the region, fortunately covering a period of less than 500 years. We adopted the French method of *histoire raisonée*. We finally set up here in Montreal at the Centre for Developing Areas Study of McGill where we enjoyed the support of a great number of Caribbean graduate students. Edwin Carrington shared the role with Adlith Brown, Noel Boissiere, Ainsworth Harewood, Phillipe Hein, Gerard Dedestyre, De Lisle Worrell, and other now well-known professionals. We entitled our study *Externally Propelled Industrialization and Growth: Models of Plantation Economy*. It was an extremely ambitious project but we soon saw it as more than the work of a lifetime; and so it would prove in ways not always intended.

The departure we made from the ideas of earlier practitioners lay in the designation "quasi-staple" we applied to such manufacturing activity and output as were beginning to appear during the 1950s and 1960s. That is to say, we doubted they were making the difference. They exhibited the same limits on transformation that had bedeviled the old natural resource-based staple exports. The manufacturing sector had been widely expected to introduce a new dynamic into the old economy, as it had done under the Smithian and Ricardian conditions of eighteenth- and early nineteenth-century England from which Professor Arthur Lewis had explicitly drawn his insights about economic and industrial development. Indeed, in the accounting framework we devised to help the exposition of an economic theory specific to the region, we included a "new dynamic sector." However, the limitations on that sector's performance were underscored in the inter-industry table by an array of empty cells reflecting the tendency of new firms neither to create and expand markets for their supply nor to engender structural interdependence in their relation with firms that were older.

We came to realize that the macro development model, which relied upon unlimited supplies of labour to flow from agriculture into manufacturing at a constant wage-rate had to be entirely re-configured. Or it had to be abandoned altogether for several reasons. First, the legacy of the Caribbean plantation had made nonsense of any meaningful relationship between agriculture and industry. There was simply no sector that could be usefully described as agriculture, enjoying the participation of farmers as distinct from cultivators, and possessing resources it could be induced by sustained investment to transfer to other sectors in order to facilitate its own internal development as well as the reconstruction of the economy. There existed only the plantation, with the stunted activities in its shadow, that was both agriculture and industry all at once, functioning in an institutional setting specific to itself. The dynamic counterpoint lay in the links – or absence of them – between the staple sector or the plantation (later termed the "offshore" sector) and the largely nonexistent residentiary or domestic sector (later called the "inshore" sector), each of which displayed properties that made their relationship the strategic and most fertile contradiction in the whole scheme. This is the feature that the great number of bearers of orthodox Ricardian, and now North Atlantic, economic theory seem specially unequipped or unwilling even to notice.

At the micro level, the distinguishing feature of business in the staple sector was its seemingly innate inability to transfer or switch resources, whether among firms offshore within the sector itself or between offshore and onshore firms. It is this immobility, or rigidity, in the movement of resources, initially including even pure labour power, that justifies the designation of the traditional export sector as "offshore." For all practical purposes, any given firm operated as if it were wholly out of the country, and save for the activity of monetizing natural resources by pressing them into production for export, it had almost no contact with the economic environment that was in theory its host. Firm and sector of this genre were pervasive. They could in no way be regarded as possessing the textbook character captured in the popular description "enclave."

Resource immobility stemmed from two founding characteristics of the post-Columbus Caribbean. First, there was the regime of slavery under which labour was in effect the main item of capital. This regime imposed the need to operate every business as if it were a "total institution," meaning a unit socially self-contained and economically self-sufficient. Second, the investor or planter being typically absentee – and the worker being invariably enslaved in a barracoon – planting was not devoted to the provisioning of households that would have satisfied the Aristotelian condition for being the basis of an authentic economy. The Caribbean economy was indeed the antithesis of the Aristotelian model. It thoroughly and completely specialized in exports and depended on imports for all its own consumption and investment needs. John Stuart Mill is famous for having declared the West Indies not an economy but the place England had chosen to produce certain commodities it needed. The region therefore possessed no small, or even micro medium enterprises with a domestic orientation. This implied that the multinational or joint-stock corporation was equally the dominant, typical, and representative firm: based overseas, tied to a head office in another country, and not inclined to take part in the formation of local markets or to form any linkages, backward or forward.

The closed nature of the firm and its corollary in the absence of markets and in the essential immobility of resources are the key to this economy's inherent incapacity: its ability to grow without ever undergoing or affecting transformation. When export earnings were high and the terms of trade favourable, it expanded and generated immense riches in terms of factor income going abroad, measuring super profits, computed, denominated, and realized in foreign exchange. By contrast, when conditions were less than favourable, unless the economy somehow acquired enough flexibility to admit movement of such strategic resources as entrepreneurial visioning, design of new business, and penetration or conquest of foreign markets for the purpose of inventing a viable new inshore sector, it had no option. It could not but consume its capital for current uses and to adopt a variety of devices that spelled short-run maladjustment and long-run stagnation.

To the extent that the business culture of the dominant firm influenced the less significant firms that typically came into existence inshore, whenever difficult conditions offshore created openings, the Ricardian yeoman farmer, family manufacturer or industrialist, whom the textbook model had assumed to be the prime agent of industrial development, simply did not fit. In sum, neither the macro nor the micro model could be usefully applied, though they necessarily constituted a piece in their own historical context. The expectation that foreign business could be invited and induced by sundry incentives to supply the scarce or absent resources of capital, know-how, and markets was hopelessly misplaced. Besides, the assumption that labour could be somehow persuaded to accept wage levels that permitted the classical "shift to profits" in pursuit of more rapid accumulation could only have been heroic. In the aftermath of self-government and independence, highly unionized labour was too acutely conscious of the experience it had been obliged to endure under the slave and colonial regimes of ancestral vintage. On all counts then, the model Kari and I had inherited drove us into an almost feverish search.

Students of West Indian economic thought recognize that the work of Sir Arthur Lewis was our point of departure. The challenge was clear. It was not merely to revise the strategies we had adopted for economic planning, management, and administration under the new-found conditions of self-determination and self-government that for the very first time dictated truly active roles for the public sector, for and on behalf of the home population. We also found ourselves needing to convert the economic history to economic theory by reviewing such offerings as Lewis's 1947 *An Economic Plan for Jamaica* and his *Labour in the West Indies*, published a decade earlier by the Fabian Society, after the establishment of the West Indies Royal (Moyne) Commission to investigate the region-wide labour riots of 1935–38. Both documents had planted seeds for public policy for decades to come.

In William Demas, Lewis would soon discover a successor of the calibre he deserved. The distinguished West Indian of the next generation passionately shared Lewis's view that small size made a single market and a Caribbean customs union or community imperative. He went further and argued the case at length in his book conceived, researched, and published here at McGill with much support and encouragement from Kari. Demas twice came to sojourn in Montreal. He came first to deliver the lectures on which the book was based and later to teach one of Kari's courses while we pursued our common research. *The Economics of Development in Small Countries with Special Reference to the Caribbean* took the first step toward an empirically based homegrown theory. That was its great merit. Demas put the accent on the admittedly important natural factor of resource endowment. We preferred to lend precedence to the human factor of institutions and culture that we thought decisive.

As director of the Economic Planning Unit of the Government of Trinidad and Tobago, Demas also agreed with Lewis on a strategic role for active government. He later followed his mentor in the role of President of the Caribbean Development Bank. What Demas did not find himself moved to do was follow through on the macroeconomic questions Lewis had raised in his seminal Manchester University piece, "Economic Development with Unlimited Supplies of Labour."[1] In some ways the responsibility fell to us to fashion a theory of growth and transformation that was cogent, comprehensive, and whole. Lewis had of course developed his interpretations as an academic and scholar in England. After his Cambridge studies, Demas, however, was from the start of his career thrown into a policy and management role in West Indian institutions. Doubtless this hands-on experience holds clues to his opus and orientation, theoretical and practical. His macroeconomics were greatly influenced by the single most important policy challenge of our time: in the aftermath of the 1930s upheaval, the requirement that Caribbean governments deliver an adequate level of employment at a living wage.

In this regard, Dudley Seers, the Oxford statistician and economist, had considerable influence on regional thinking through his research and writings and the consultant role he played in the planning divisions of Jamaica and Trinidad. Seers's "The Mechanism of an Open Petroleum Economy"[2] focused on distribution aspects. It tracked the transfers from offshore to inshore, the size of government revenue and the wages fund that it effectively constituted, and its impact in terms of jobs created by government expenditure. Here too, as with the Lewis model we named "industrialization by invitation," the wage rate was a critical variable. With the energy sector of Trinidad and Tobago, offshore activity tended to become increasingly capital intensive, meaning that any given wages fund implied an ever-diminishing capacity to create jobs. These immediate and delicate concerns explain Seers's emphasis on the shorter term.

At the same time, his work displayed a keen interest in the longer-term effect of multinational forms of business organization on income and employment.[3] It also drew attention to perhaps the most fundamental issue of all: the dangers of an economics simply transposed from the textbook case of early industrialization in a few countries to the great number of new states seeking to transform their economies by their own devices. What did such an insensitive imposition of a paradigm imply for policy perceptions and management choices?[4]

Both these papers without doubt sharpened our professional awareness in the region. While priorities for practitioners were undoubtedly set by Seers's vision for the shorter term, our agenda was framed by considerations of the longer term. Though we were facilitated by the compact accounting schema Seers had devised for annual forecasts of revenue, expenditure, and employment, we also brought ideas of our own. Levitt had worked on input-output tables for the Maritime provinces and had collaborated closely with Terry Gigantes of Statistics Canada and Matuchevski of Laval University. Best had had years as a national accounts Fellow with Dr Carleen O'Loughlin at ISER, Mona. In the end we developed a full social accounting matrix meant to capture aspects Seers had argued for on the reasoning that they invariably shaped the character of both inter-industry and value-added flows.

At the same time, we never shifted our gaze away from Lewis, who had a sharp exchange over his plan for Jamaica with Professor Frederick Benham, then adviser to the colonial development and welfare scheme London had devised for the West Indies after the West Indies Royal Commission Report. In his response Lewis had offered the first empirical explanation for labour's well-known tendency to reduce the offer of its services to the plantation sector whenever wage levels rose. Lewis had demonstrated that the so-called "backward-sloping supply curve of labour" involved a straightforward, rational, and unmysterious reallocation of time between paid work and the sweat equity that could be accumulated on the family holding. Prior to that refutation of their prejudices, employers seemed partial to the idea of the lazy worker with limited material needs. It furnished them the rationale for keeping wages to the barest minimum.

Kari and I delved into the history that had led Lewis to his theory of the Caribbean labour market. We realized that the collapse of the old slave regime during the first half of the nineteenth century – and the abrupt change of social context it had brought about – dictated for the researcher a model similar to but in some ways very different from what was called for by the plantation economy of earlier vintage. We settled for a schema involving three separate interpretations, each with its corresponding model representing successive stages of history. The Pure Plantation Economy constituted Model I and was meant to cover the period 1640 to 1840. The Plantation Economy Modified constituted Model II and covered the period 1840 to 1940; while Model III described the Plantation Economy Further Modified, covering the period 1940 to the present. We envisaged but never formalized a Model IV that might conceivably identify conditions when the old strategy of industrialization by invitation would have been effectively displaced.

In point of fact, some such conceptual staging had been triggered by a discussion of the middle period, the West Indian nineteenth century that did not end until 1940. We had considered the Lewis analysis of the efforts post-emancipation society had made to face up to the imperatives of free labour. In a brainstorming we had with our UWI colleague Alister McIntyre in 1964 at the St Augustine Campus, when I was on loan there from Mona teaching, we ended up with copious notes and diagrams that were to fuel what was to follow. Unfortunately these working papers were destroyed in the Tapia House fire at 22 Cipriani Boulevard, Port of Spain on 24 January 1982.

Once slavery was done, the highest priority of free labour lay in modifying the old economy by legitimating and entrenching a second sector inshore. The aim was to consolidate the new, domestic or residentiary sector, comprised of peasant farms, cultivator plots, and independent craftsmen who emerged as the plantation broke down offshore. It was however still necessary to earn great amounts of foreign exchange to pay the bills in an economy no longer totally but still excessively specialized in exports and sporting a pronounced taste for imports. In part, this meant wage work; in part it implied agricultural production for the home market to displace exports and save foreign exchange. Above all, it dictated the addition of minor agriculture staples to the major one, sugar.

The precise mandate for this new sector was to refuse the externally propelled character of the economy – to reduce its vulnerability to global price and policy shocks. The virtue of Lewis's diagnosis at the turn to the 1950s was that it underlined the sector's ultimate failure to introduce any such abiding new dynamics. His piece on the peasantry is an education in itself. He put the failure to transform down to several factors. First, population growth cancelled the effect of capital accumulation and technical progress and prevented development on the intensive frontier. Second, limited land availability scuttled progress on the extensive frontier. Third, the wanton laissez-faire policies of the colonial regime were zealous about not improving land distribution and landholding arrangements, education and extension services, infrastructure or the climate for investment.

This failure of course showed up in chronic unemployment and induced adjustments in the form of withdrawal of women from the labour market, external migration to Central and North America, internal migration to the towns to set up petty trades marked by very low productivity and incomes, and most important, mounting so much pressure on the land that output would rise if more people were to leave.

The threshold of the late 1930s had struck the professional observer's imagination. Lewis's prescriptions emphasized spending from two quarters. First, there was foreign aid to fund public capital. Second, foreign direct investment to establish manufacturing meant to deliver output not only for export but also for the home market, as we have seen, in the context of a customs union, still being pursued today by CARICOM under the leadership of Demas and the rubric of the Caribbean Single Market and Economy (CSME).

As suggested, the dynamics were of English vintage. The (initially) foreign firm would lead the process of expansion to generate new employment and higher national income. Profits would expand the firm's share of total income. Reminiscent of Ricardo's world, ploughing back was expected to raise the rate of accumulation. Benefits would be passed on to agriculture through enhanced demand for its output and wider opportunity to upgrade technology, improve organization, and raise productivity as labour migrated. The savings rate of domestic firms would also rise, permitting entrepreneurs to emerge and to cross over to industry confident of the necessary finance. If this seemed to resemble the process with which students of the first industrial revolution were fully familiar, Professor Lewis's ideas nevertheless involved an important departure, perhaps as important as that of Keynes' General Theory, then adding a wider post-war success to the qualified gains it had made mostly in pre-war North America.

Lewis's thinking clarified a distinction that was then still hazy. On the one hand, there was essentially seasonal or cyclical unemployment in the industrial countries. Depression was set against an abundance of all factors of production, needing only effective demand to induce activity and employment. On the other hand, the unemployment that existed in the primary producing countries was chronic and structural. If the supply of labour could be assumed to be unlimited it was because plant, equipment, and infrastructure were also absent and markets for output still had to be called into existence. These were two entirely different situations and Dr Lewis had made the position plain in the *Caribbean Review* essays where he had set out his scheme for attracting the other resources by wooing and fawning on investors.

And yet, in his program for "Industrialization of the British West Indies," modelled to an extent on his "Industrial Development in Puerto Rico," Lewis found himself standing perilously in two places at once. His frames of reference unwittingly joined the England of the late eighteenth and early nineteenth centuries to the mid-twentieth-century West Indies. This led to diagnostic and prescriptive complications, complications that hold clues to the work that developed thereafter. Certainly, studies by Kari and me, and by George Beckford,

Norman Girvan, Owen Jefferson, and others with whom we collaborated closely, owe their orientation to a perception that here was a picture needing to be cleared up. Here was one of the founders of the economics of development who would be justly recognized as a master of the art. With Raoul Prebisch, Hans Singer, and Gunnar Myrdal, Lewis had been among the first to raise the alarm over the gains from international trade accruing to primary producers. These concerns, very much the substance of his early work, fixed him as a West Indian, true to his origins in an economy created by absentee, direct investment, and in many ways thereafter its creature, vulnerable to a fault to external shocks.

Lewis's initial concerns also implied that studies in trade theory and policy needed to go beyond their restricted postulates and the much too comfortable notion of comparative advantage. The attention Lewis devoted to the theory of economic growth and to the wealth of nations did, in truth and in fact, help to steer the discipline toward issues of resource creation as much as those of resource allocation. His was a just claim that his work was returning us to the classics. He would however also select and use tools from neo-classical economics, and he would adopt a stance of deliberate overlap with the Keynesians of the generation inclined to make exports rather than investment the driving force in some "open" economies. In the critique of the models by Levitt and Best coming from still younger generations, such fertile promiscuity would once again be the subject of comment.

We are happy to have been in such august company. There is no denying that Lewis is the figure with whose *œuvre* all West Indian economics begins. There were indeed secrets he had failed to unearth, but so often he provided the touchstone. He was prompter and promoter of Gisela Eisner's seminal work, *Jamaica 1830–1930*.[5] No study so illumines the path by which peasant entrepreneurship arose with great vigour only to lose its momentum, thanks to the rigidities of the modified plantation regime and its obsession with staple exports, sugar in particular. And yet the Lewis program of industrialization neglected the central problem, the stunting effect of staple exports on residentiary activity.

The plantation was an economic and business institution different in kind from both the classical and the neo-classical firm. If it was eager to promote expansion, it also shared the priority the mercantilist gave to foreign exchange, to a high staple share of total output, and to an intra-firm division of labour favouring staple export specialization. Countries that received foreign investment, routinely exercised the option against import displacement and even against import replacement. Above all, the plantation discriminated against dynamic new exports. Nor was such bias independent of that form of business organization which gave precedence to externally based corporations.

Here is the legacy with which the post-World War II generation had to work. Levitt and Best were at first perhaps too close on the heels of the master. With distance we got a much better picture. The lucidity and point of the Lewis proposals for industrial development, the range of his vision, the issues he opened up are universally acknowledged. They confirm an *opus* without which it would have been many times more difficult to arrive at an organic interpretation. Kari and I had to draw on Caribbean experience and regional materials. We also had to adopt the institutional premises that were shared by the humanities in particular and were able to support a fully extradisciplinary view covering the politics, sociology, psychology and philosophy all at once. This is the direction in which we needed to go after our initial exposition had focused on a matter that was almost wholly economic.

In terms of diagnosis and prescription, Lewis survives as a remarkable transitional figure who had settled his paradigm at the turn from the 1930s. Independence not only demanded autonomous theory, it also provided the experience from which practical insight and hard information could be drawn. The challenge of sifting the modalities of chronic surplus labour also compelled us to spell out the macro- and microeconomics in all their fullness. The new work attributes the failure to transform the economy and to make full employment possible to two factors, both of human origin. First is the character of the firm prevalent at the micro level. Second is the institutional regime of resource allocation and income appropriation at the macro level to which, from its inception, the externally propelled economy was subject and the operation of which has become its own entrenched "culture."

In their engagement with markets and their involvement in structural interdependence, emerging firms inshore tend to adopt the profile of their established counterparts offshore. The effect is only to introduce new rigidities. Old rigidities already described a tendency for the economy, when enjoying a period of plenty, to acquire encumbrances in the form of offshore commitments to meet foreign claims. Such commitments were almost impossible to sustain when terms of trade degenerated and times turned sour, from a Golden Age, in fact, to Gall and Wormwood. The effect was to reduce the current national income available either for redistribution inshore or for deployment on strategic spending to build a viable new order.

For their part, the newer rigidities take the form of certain encumbrances the inshore economy acquires in the upswing and in the times of great abundance. Again there is a burgeoning of activities incapable of sustaining themselves unless offshore operations provide them with foreign exchange, famously the scarce resource. To the extent that such activities do not engage domestic supply markets or engender structural interdependence, they have little difficulty effecting an early takeoff, thereby leaving to lag behind, or even crowding out, precisely those activities that promise transformation. This is due not so much to the size of their claims as to their place in the sequence. This culture of taking the short view in the sense of promoting business that has no long-term future but can gain investment precedence must be seen as deriving from a long historical experience and tradition.

Over the centuries, the Caribbean economy has counted on bouts of expansion over the longer term. These have admittedly been punctuated by intervals of contraction or stagnation; but they have been made repeatedly possible either by unprogrammed revivals in the price of mature staples or by the discovery of new natural resources followed by new external investment, improved technology, different outputs, and higher export earnings. It is this confidence in an ultimate recovery, by whatever means, that is perhaps at the root of what only seems like business risk-aversion but might well be rational calculation for the firm by itself, if not for the economy as a whole.

At the micro level, encumbrances that mortgage future earnings may be worth risking; but their effect can only be diabolical in the wider macro context where it is imperative to consider the whole range of booming and slumping sector effects of natural resource exploitation and not simply those consequences economists popularly link to the "Dutch Disease"[6] and the impact of exchange rate appreciation.

This suggests that perhaps the most important aspect of the studies by Levitt and Best is that they went beyond the conventional issue of the gains from production and trade and the distribution of gross product between investors offshore and the national population inshore – or among the latter. Emotional appeal notwithstanding, it has been much less interesting to find out who has remained poor in the unequal exchange than to fathom the ways and means by which the economy as a whole has remained stunted for so long. This is again a question of a long and short view. It was in the mechanics of "encumbrances" that we found the vital clue to persistent underperformance. It was in that same connection that we first glimpsed the importance of culture along with institutions. We were required to transcend the economics and to see the challenge in a multidisciplinary or extra-disciplinary light.

We aimed at a theory of resource employment, resource mobility, and resource remuneration but in the end that seemed only a beginning. We realized that the issue of resource immobility had been posed in 1947 by Henry Wallich in his study of the Cuban economy entitled *Monetary*

Problems of an Export Economy,[7] itself drawing on rich historical documentation by Fernando Ortiz in *Cuban Counterpoint: Tobacco and Sugar*,[8] and Ramiro Guerra in *Sugar and Society in the Caribbean.*[9] Wallich saw with great clarity that there existed a very special brand of immobility in the Cuban case where soaring sugar prices often generated a great fund of financial resources, impossible to translate into real ones. Huge incomes became available, but they did not result from any intervention whatsoever by business organization or productive activity.

Converting the opportunity required the business resources available to sugar to transfer their attention to activity that was not landbased. That no such thing ever happened served to establish the issue. Periods of abundance created opportunity but were laconically unrequited by business activity, whether local or foreign. Productive resources were simply tied up or not flexible enough. That it was not a straightforward matter of stretched capacity makes it necessary for us to focus on the specific character and culture of firms. Aware of this cultural dimension, we attempted to align our theory to the analysis the historians provided, raising the issue of hypotheses that had to be testable and tested but not directly answering the question of whether by historical or economic methods.

Responding to the dual requirement, we attempted to underpin theory and history with the corresponding framework for national and social accounting we had developed (as noted, with not a few borrowings from Seers – who ironically was unusually worried about the cultural lag in economics and in national accounting[10]). He was anxious that new models and accounting schemes should capture culturally conditioned oddities of behaviour as well as the institutional setting. With our *Model of Pure Plantation Economy*, which we completed in 1968, we hoped we had met the principal requirements. We had provided a more than plausible theoretical explanation of the way the economy functioned – in its purest and simplest form.

For precisely the reason that the post-emancipation nineteenth century witnessed most of the experiments in diversification undertaken in the region, Model II proved too complex a challenge for the short run. For Model III, we cast our exposition in the guise mostly of the fully elaborated accounting framework and laid the basis for future endeavours. This in sum is the substance of Levitt and Best's joint effort. It is quite a handful but it does raise the question of what we have done since, having left the academic and intellectual community with the core statement only in four multilith volumes. The bulk of George Beckford's and Norman Girvan's findings and interpretations has been widely aired.[11] But ours, which constitutes the burden of the new theoretical and empirical work, remains unpublished.

Kari has lamented that her own perfectionism was what inhibited us from putting out the sundry volumes, even as they were in 1968. In reviewing our own collaboration, in the inaugural edition of the journal of the Association of Caribbean Economists, *Marronage*,[12] she describes her attempt to make the national and social accounting models operational in Trinidad and Tobago. We had hoped that not only would the statistical picture have yielded flows for testing but also that it would itself have disseminated much of the story. That too was not to be.

WHY ARE WE ONLY NOW GOING TO PUBLISH?

Kari has remarked that I had my own reasons for not proceeding to publish in book or monograph form. She is more right than she knows. The first thing I can say is that no sooner had I returned to Trinidad from Montreal in October 1968 than I acquired priorities I had in no way anticipated. But it would be a great error to conclude that my reluctance to go to what many saw as the finish had anything at all to do with my engagement for a decade and a half in public life and political competition. From the very beginning, I told Kari, and I kept insisting, that the task of putting out a book was low on my personal and professional agenda. I must say that openly now so that she can confirm it.

As it turned out, it was only until 1976 that I remained a conventional academic in the UWI and in principle not free to change my priorities. That was however in the midst of an ongoing upheaval among the country's urban youth with its centre, moreover, among many of my own students on campus. Certainly it was that uprising that swept me summarily into the Tapia House Group and later into the Tapia House Movement, our electoral party. But my refusal – indeed my inability – to embark on publishing sprang from much deeper urges and impulses that would become clear only much later. They were the manifestations of an epistemic concept I could hardly expect even my most intimate friends to take as more than rationalization, even given abundant indicators of the way I could have been expected to react and respond to events, indicators that have become increasingly abundant since.

Not only did those turbulent years of the 1970s compel me at first to voice in a tentative fashion and then to act on my convictions regarding the link between being, knowing, and acting; they also made me marvel, even as I was not surprisingly pained over the strange ways by which intimate friends and collaborators both influence and fail to influence one another. I acquired much fresh insight into the routes by which the wider community, including the narrower academic and intellectual community, learns – and fails to learn – from what is done, said, and written. The resulting divergence of agendas did not disrupt the flow of friendship, admiration, and love but it did colour perception, change our body language, and in sum it did matter.

I found myself aghast at the stolid and even self-righteous incapacity of many old friends and collaborators from the New World Group to realize that our founding of the Tapia House Group on 14 November 1968, was the only conceivable way to pre-empt the kind of unraveling we were to see in Grenada in 1983. By late 1968 New World (Trinidad) had lost interest in anything save taking office, which they mistook for power. It had been transformed into the kind of populist, apocalyptic, fake-revolutionary organization that clearly had the illusion it could dislodge Williams and PNM almost without tears.

My open decision to abandon and renounce the outfit – and to start something more along the lines of what Kari has said we had all espoused in pursuit of independent thought and Caribbean freedom – did not stop the devotees of overnight change in their tracks. But it did soon expose their intellectual bankruptcy and unbridled opportunism. We have commented pointedly on the subsequent career of their *Moko* journal and on their launching of the UNIP election party in December 1970. How can all that not confirm that Tapia and not New World (Trinidad) was assuring our continuity?

I am happy that the more than three decades since have established some things beyond doubt. At no stage did Tapia ever sacrifice intellectual or critical standards on the altar of electoral expediency. On no account did we place office before the elevation of political standards for which the absolutely indispensable ingredients could only have been personal integrity, pervasive intellectual life, full freedom of expression, and unrelieved discourse. The orientation of the Tapia newspaper from its very inception, the type of campaign we conducted in the election of 1976, our issue in 1977 of the *T&T Review*, and our founding in 1978 of the T&T Institute of the West Indies all attest to our objectives. They testify to the long view we have invariably taken.

I was at first appalled that so many friends displayed an attitude that put the highest value on successful street mobilization, easy persuasion of uninformed opinion, and by extension on the deceptive political success boasted by our rivals. I was for a while taken aback by postures that simply pooh-poohed and cold-shouldered Tapia but found little difficulty supporting or adhering to groups, movements, and parties across the Caribbean that made great play of radical transformation but have since sadly exited the stage, leaving neither architecture, ideas nor organization relevant to our future. We received some quite extraordinary proposals about people we should align with or about procedures or stances we should adopt toward our paper or our political practice. Not a few of us allowed ourselves to be taken in by Burnham simply because he had moved on the bauxite multinationals and had proclaimed he was for food, clothes, and shelter for the "masses." Michael Manley appealed to the regional imagination and consumed the energies of large numbers. We did not until later discover that his socialism was bogus and could, at the drop of a hat, be converted into liberal capitalism. We did not see that too much of the impetus was provided by the traditional self-love and patronage of the Caribbean maximum leader corrupted by the ethos of permanent central power and one-man rule.

I later came to see these other views as manifestations of precisely the epistemic divergences and differences of approach that surfaced under the conditions of extreme stress at the turn to the 1970s. In extenuation I must add that the last time I saw George Beckford before he passed away, in characteristic generosity he told me how much he admired "your patience." I had never understood his distance from Tapia – he never even read the paper – but I think he finally saw how far-sighted we had been; and how we had tried to maintain the integrity of the New World vision. It took Kari a great deal longer. She had first to put her finger in the wound and to witness the collapse of both the politics and economics in the region.

I cannot deny that, in thirty years, we did not put our materials out in some combination of books and monographs. Not only for Kari's sake, I have now put systems in place which I expect to make the omission good relatively soon. The Trinidad and Tobago Institute of the West Indies has only now reached the stage where publication of that genre forms part of our normal ongoing program – without obliging us to incur prohibitive costs or to run into too many complications over donors we could risk taking funding from. Though the wider availability of our results cannot have been less than a real consideration, I have at no stage been diverted by the chorus willing me to subscribe to the West Indian miracle of print.

And yet I'm not sure that what has happened can be judged as error or accident. On my part, it did involve calculation, at least in some measure. Over the years I have not simply refrained from adopting the priorities of others with different insights and interests. I have indeed been doing something else that I have all along wanted to do, something more important to me than any sole academic publication. I hope the evidence of my statement will one day confirm that I have been zealous, perhaps single minded, in disseminating, not just the results of our work but the whole epistemic method that had in the first place led us to embark upon the project and to surround it with organization in the form of New World Group as a West Indian party and not simply a study group of dissenting economists. I have also deepened and extended the analysis as can probably be judged from the exposition in this piece.

Above all, I have systematically widened the interpretation to cover not merely the economics but the sociology, government, and politics as well. These were compulsions visited upon me by praxis in an evolving situation demanding more and deeper comprehension of Caribbean reality. I do not share the apocalyptic notion that the world is waiting for our statement or that we are somehow going to finish the work with some definitive Model IV. What we publish must emerge organically and when it will from the whole range of our commitments and priorities. These include the issue of our journal with its mandate to serve the intellectual and critical tradition by the constant mobilization over decades of researchers, thinkers, writers, readers, editors, etc. I have absolutely no apologies. We have simply paid the price of so many of us deluding ourselves and going off on tangents, withholding resources from the essentials and the mainstream.

To my mind, the great paradox is that not many of the economists and scholars, not even those with privileged access to what we had completed as early as 1968–71, have exhibited any recognition of what, in substance and in method, the work implies, least of all for the various disciplines in an extra-disciplinary perspective. Nor have we showed much sensitivity to its bearing on our whole world view. I have alluded mostly to the political postures. It surprises me, however, that once I parted company, few expressions of our thought survived and only in fragments of thoroughly unsatisfactory courses taught at the UWI, still somehow never converted into any cogent reconfiguration of the crazy and indefensible macro- and microeconomics we'd inherited. The one honourable initiative I know is the attempt by William Demas to have Kari lead a team to reformulate the national accounts of Trinidad and Tobago but that was of course aborted for reasons we should explore in their fullness.

In my purview are not only the colleagues whose hostility was scarcely disguised but intimate collaborators whose favour we have enjoyed without equivocation. About them I intend no complaint and certainly no indictment. I have simply wondered why CARICOM for instance has never proceeded to employ our accounting framework for the purpose of interpretations and measurements common to all the integration partners and required for making the economies comparative and additive. This is clearly not a case where a neglect to publish in one particular form has withheld vital information. Quite the contrary, it clinches the issue as epistemic. Is it that we needed some sort of authorized version?

This brings us to the West Indian pathology of philosopher-king and scholar revolutionary. Alas, it is still the only model we subscribe to, although we may not even be conscious of our devotion to Caribbean politics in its most traditional incarnation. I can only say that my determination to repudiate that conventional ethos ruled out option after option for me. Every kind of charlatanry was put to me by collaborators and associates who had no idea whatsoever what Tapia or Best was about. There is plenty of evidence to suggest this as the source of much of the disgruntlement over Tapia and over so much else.

The great lesson is that humans do not learn simply by being told, informed, or even by having high mutual regard. These things help but there remains the matter of psychology, culture, and inter-personal politics that govern receptivity and effective communication. After all is said and done, the important thing might be that over the years we have sustained better than professional collegialities. Kari and I have never ceased to be friends able to talk frankly. We've also grown. And we've survived to make many things good.

NOTES

1 W.A. Lewis, "Economic Development with Unlimited Supplies of Labour," *Manchester School* 22 (May 1954):139–91.

2 Dudley Seers, "The Mechanism of an Open Economy," *Social and Economic Studies* 13 (no. 2, 1964):233–542.

3 Dudley Seers, "Big Companies and Small Countries. A practical Proposal," *Kyklos* 16 (1963):599–608.

4 Dudley Seers, "Limitations of the Special Case," *Bulletin of the Oxford Institute of Economics and Statistics* 1963 (May).

5 Gisela Eisner, *Jamaica 1830–1930. A Study in Economic Growth* (Manchester: Manchester University Press, 1961).

6 The Dutch Disease applies to countries which, like Holland when it was favoured by the huge reserves of oil in the North Sea, find themselves with a superabundance of foreign exchange and wildly appreciating currencies that render their tradeable goods sectors uncompetitive – thereby biasing and skewing investments.

7 Henry Wallich, *Monetary Problems of an Export Economy, The Cuban Experience, 1914–1947* (Cambridge: Harvard University Press, 1960).

8 Fernando Ortiz, *Cuban Counterpoint: Tobacco and Sugar,* trans. H. de Onis (New York: Knopf, 1947).

9 Ramiro Guerra, *Sugar and Society in the Caribbean: An Economic History of Cuban Agriculture* (New Haven: Yale University Press, 1964).

10 Dudley Seers, *The Cultural Lag in Economics* (Sussex: Institute of Development Studies, University of Sussex, August 1978).

11 George Beckford, *Persistent Poverty: Underdevelopment in the Plantation Economies of the Third World* (New York: Oxford University Press, 1972). For example, see Norman Girvan, "The Development of Dependency Economics in the Caribbean and Latin America: Review and Comparison," *Social and Economic Studies* 22 (no. 1, March 1973).

12 Kari Polanyi Levitt, "My Collaboration with Lloyd Best," *Marronage* 1 (no. 1, September 1998):1–26.

7 Kari Polanyi Levitt and the Theory of Plantation Economy in Contemporary Perspective

NORMAN GIRVAN

"Whatever happened to Plantation Economy?" a student in my graduate course on theories of development recently asked. We had completed a review of dependency theory, in which the theories of Plantation Economy developed by Lloyd Best, Kari Polanyi-Levitt, and George Beckford had figured prominently. The student wondered why he had not been exposed to this work in his undergraduate training. He thought it was relevant to an understanding of contemporary issues in development and the world economy.

In the ensuing discussion I sensed a revival of interest in non-mainstream economic thinking, particularly political economy and analysis of institutions and relations of power. The catalyst for this was the world economic crisis of 1997–98 and the failure of neoliberal thinking to anticipate and explain events or provide satisfactory policy responses. The students were casting around for other ways to understand the world they were living in. The intractable economic and social problems of Jamaica after twenty years of neoliberal structural adjustment was another factor contributing to their dissatisfaction.

The occasion of a Kari Levitt Festschrift provides a timely opportunity for a reappraisal of the theory of Plantation Economy some thirty years after its first appearance (Best & Levitt 1969). Fortunately the necessary materials are becoming available. *Marronage*, the journal of the Association of Caribbean Economists, has published its first issue containing the proceedings of a conference marking the twenty-fifth anniversary of the work (Pantin & Mahabir 1998). Kari and her colleague Michael Witter have already edited a publication in honour of George "Gbeck" Beckford, another pioneer in the field (Levitt & Witter 1996). Kari has also completed the editing of Beckford's collected papers for publication.[1] There remains, however, a great need to publish the original Best-Levitt essay on Plantation Economy.

I write as one of the members of the original team assembled by Lloyd and Kari in the late 1960s, and one whose work over the past three decades has been enormously influenced by their studies of Plantation Economy.[2] In this paper – which is my own personal tribute to Kari – I make some observations on the work in the perspective of the last thirty years.

OVERVIEW OF THE MODELS OF PLANTATION ECONOMY

The Best-Levitt Plantation Economy studies sought to identify the structural constraints on the growth and transformation of Caribbean economies that arise from the historical legacy of the plantation system and the pervasiveness of plantation-type institutions in the contemporary economy in the form of the multinational corporation (MNC). Their studies also intended to specify the features of a self-reliant, self-sustaining Caribbean economy that functions in the interests of the majority of the population.

The analysis drew from a wide range of economists and historians and a variety of intellectual traditions. From Marshallian microeconomics it drew the analytical device of the representative firm, which in this context was the plantation in the hinterland economy. From Keynesian macroeconomics it borrowed mechanisms of income creation and multiplier effects, which were held to take place largely in the metropole. The structuralist flavour of the Best-Levitt analysis – dependence on a single export crop that is reproduced over time in a dynamic of growth without development – was strongly influenced by the work of Dudley Seers and the Latin American school, especially Celso Furtado.

Drawing on the work of the American anthropologist Charles Wagley, Best and Levitt developed their typology of hinterlands of conquest, of settlement, and of exploitation, the plantation economy being an example of the last. From a detailed study of the work of the West Indian historians Eric Williams, Elsa Goviea, and Douglas Hall, they took their specifications of the "Pure Plantation Economy" of the period of chattel slavery. They refined their analysis of the impact of the export staple by drawing on the insights of Innis and Mel Watkins in the Canadian context. And Leontief's input-output analysis was adapted to construct an accounting framework for Pure Plantation

Economy (Model I) and Plantation Economy Further Modified (Model III), meant to be an empirical frame for data collection and analysis. The work was eclectic in the best meaning of the word, blending a variety of analytical approaches, or paradigms, to produce a distinct model of its own.

To this blend Kari brought a tradition of humane, transdisciplinary political economy that perhaps only a child of the great Karl Polanyi could have had so deeply in the very marrow of her intellectual bones. She brought her grounding in the staple theories of the Canadian economy, her own original work on the MNC in Canada, and her skills in input-output analysis that had been honed in her statistical work on the Canadian Atlantic provinces. Lloyd Best for his part brought not only his skills as an economist but also his deep knowledge of Caribbean economic history together with an absolute irreverence for established ways of looking at the world and a total determination to conduct unique and original theorizing.

This fertile collaboration influenced a whole generation of Caribbean students and scholars[3] and I count myself as one of its principal beneficiaries. Indeed it is still my view that the plantation economy models of Best, Levitt, and Beckford provide the single most powerful set of expository devices for explaining the persistence of underdevelopment and dependence and the dysfunctional behaviour of different agents in contemporary Caribbean economies.

That said, this occasion has stimulated me to reflect and to make some observations on the Best-Levitt model, or series of models, in the light of economic experience and additions to knowledge in the past thirty years. Most of these observations relate to the Best-Levitt models themselves although I also refer to the closely related work of Beckford.

GENERALITY VS SPECIFICITY

First, my sense is that there has been a marked increase in the tension between the generality of the plantation models and the specificity of the experiences of individual islands and territories. The Caribbean now contains a number of small island dependencies and mini-states that specialize in exports of services and have relatively high per capita incomes. The more populous islands and the Guianas, on the other hand, still have large agricultural sectors and relatively low per capita incomes. Between the two are oil-rich Trinidad and Tobago, economically diversified and relatively well-off Barbados, the banana-producing Windards islands, and industrialized Puerto Rico. Divergent trajectories of development make it more and more difficult to deal with the Caribbean experience within the framework of a single, all-encompassing paradigm.

Economic diversity within the Caribbean reflects the inequalities and uneven development characteristic of the world capitalist economy as a whole. The Plantation Economy model in fact addressed intra-Caribbean diversity. The Modified version explored the different patterns of adjustment of "mature" as compared to "new" hinterlands; and the Further Modified version discussed the "new export staples" of petroleum, bauxite, and tourism, as well as "branch-plant manufacturing." The argument was that the modified versions of Plantation Economy remained constrained by the legacy of the original pure form, that the new export staples essentially replicated the behavioural patterns of the original sugar sector, and that the MNCs are the twentieth-century version of the joint-stock trading company. Hence the theme of continuity with change – with the emphasis on continuity.

This was the source of the power and appeal of the Plantation Economy models: everything could be explained in terms of the plantation. But it may also have been a weakness. Subsequent studies of Caribbean economies and export industries show the complexity of contemporary adaptations of structures arising out of the interplay of external institutions and internal processes. The oil industry of Trinidad and Tobago, the bauxite industry of Jamaica, and the tourism industries all over the Caribbean do indeed differ widely from the original plantations in the details of their economic impact (taxation and employment, for instance), as well as in their social structure and labour relations. More and more, these industries demand analysis *sui generis* rather than in terms of a model originally based on the slave plantation. By extension, this also applies to analysis of the societies as a whole. And it probably helps to explain the waning appeal of the models to subsequent generations of Caribbean scholars in the 1980s and 1990s.

THE MODELS AS A GUIDE TO POLICY

Another question relates to the value of the models as guide to policies and strategies of transformation. This was hinted at, but never fully elaborated as an operational framework. It would presumably have been the basis for Model IV, the so-called "anti-model" (Levitt 1998:1). The hints relate to the argument that the true potential for transformation lay in what was called the "residentiary" sector, which originated in the peasant economy established in the post-Emancipation period. What exactly constituted the residentiary sector in the contemporary economy, however, was never fully specified. Is it ownership (local), race (Black/East Indian), class (peasantry/workers), market orientation (domestic) or a combination of all four? The work of George

Beckford goes further in calling for the "freeing up" of the residentiary sector, by which he meant essentially the activities of poor black people both rural and urban, including the informal economy. But some intriguing questions arise out of this position:

- When small farmers (or small producers generally) participate in production of an exported commodity such as sugar cane and bananas, this is residentiary in ownership but not in market orientation. Does this limit the potential of this activity to contribute to economic transformation?
- How can large-scale industries such as petroleum and bauxite be made "residential"? Does this not involve the role of the state?
- Are all residentiary activities to be regarded positively? What about crime and drug trafficking, for example?
- What about the issue of class – is the residentiary sector to be promoted regardless of the possible emergence of a native capitalist class that is exploitative in its labour relations and socially irresponsible in its economic practice (as in Jamaica in the 1990s)? If not, what does this imply about the role of the state?
- What about the Caribbean diaspora overseas, whose population and economic significance rivals that of the resident population – are those people not, in essence, an "overseas" residentiary sector of the Caribbean?

ROLE OF THE STATE

Best and Levitt's Plantation Economy studies did not say much about the role of the state. This figured more prominently in my own work (1970) and that of George Beckford (1972), and C.Y. Thomas (1973). During the 1970s several Caribbean governments[4] adopted policies of localization and nationalization of foreign-owned industries. It is probably true to say that these were inspired at least in part by the plantation school, though there were other contributory influences including the Cuban Revolution, the Black Power movement, Caribbean Marxism, and Third World radicalism. On the whole the results of these experiments ranged from the disappointing to the disastrous. The reasons for this included:

- opposition from established interests among the MNCs, the local private sector, and the U.S. (cases of Jamaica and Guyana)
- corruption, patronage, and political authoritarianism undermining the profitability of state-owned enterprises (especially the case of Guyana)

- absence of a coherent economic model and management (case of Jamaica in particular)
- state trying to do too much too quickly with too much money (case of oil-rich Trinidad and Tobago in the 1970s)
- internal social and political contradictions (cases of Grenada and Jamaica)

In retrospect, the advocates of statist polices (including me) were unduly optimistic about the capacity of state-owned enterprises to be agents of economic transformation, separate from the political cultural context in which they would function. However, as pointed out, Best and Levitt did not themselves advocate policies of widespread nationalization, although there were some vague references to localization.

REGIONAL ECONOMIC INTEGRATION

The studies also recommended regional economic integration as a strategy. Again the experience has been disappointing. The Caribbean Community (CARICOM), formed in 1973, did not live up to its original promise to forge a strong regional grouping with coordinated development of agriculture, industry, and natural resources. But it would be unfair to use this as evidence of the faultiness of the Plantation Economy analysis. Best and Levitt saw regional integration as a complement to changing internal structures of production and accumulation. CARICOM never went beyond liberalizing the internal economic management of intra-regional trade, and has focused much of its effort on coordinating external trade negotiations and foreign policy and on functional cooperation in social affairs.

CARICOM governments have been preoccupied with preserving and maximizing the short-term benefits of preferential trading arrangements with the metropolitan centres including Lome, the Caribbean Basin Initiative (CBI), and Caribcan. Business interests have also focused on their linkages with the developed countries. Hence policies have been constrained by the imperatives flowing from inherited structures of the plantation economy in its successive versions. The growing heterogeneity of Caribbean economies has also impeded the integration process. The tourist and service economies of CARICOM had more to lose than to gain from a strong common market, which would have mostly benefited the larger agricultural and manufacturing exporting member countries.

There have also been divergent policy agendas. In the 1970s, Trinidad and Tobago was pursuing energy-based industrialization, Jamaica was experimenting with democratic socialism and campaigning for a new international economic order, and Guyana was trying to build cooperative socialism, while Barbados was following more orthodox policies. In the 1980s, integration was undermined by the effects of structural adjustment programs, which favoured trade liberalization with the rest of the world and a retreat from interventionist policies. By the 1990s Caricom had largely embraced the new orthodoxy of open regionalism. Yet it is arguably the case that the current pressures of market globalization have reinforced the need to consolidate the Community into a coherent economic bloc in the shape of the Caricom Single Market and Economy (CSME).

CLASS AND RACE

The Plantation Economy school (and here I include George Beckford) is at its strongest when it analyzes the coincidence of class and race relations in plantation societies and the bases of ethnic antagonism in ethnically plural plantation societies like Trinidad and Tobago, Guyana, and Suriname. A good example is the case of contemporary Jamaica, which is arguably in a process of social fragmentation. On one side is a parasitic ruling class depending on the state and on financial capital and largely the product of the policies of structural adjustment and liberalization. This class was consolidated out of the remnants of the old plantation-mercantile system in Jamaica together with a new brown bourgeoisie emerging out of financial liberalization and privatization.

On the other hand is the majority black population, who experience varying degrees of social and economic exclusion. The core resides in the inner city communities in Kingston and adjacent areas, where alternative systems of economy and social authority outside the law have become established. These communities are in a state of endemic revolt against the official system of justice and politics. The attitudes of the Jamaican ruling class toward the inner city communities are for the most characterized by a mixture of indifference, contempt, and fear – which closely resemble the attitudes of the planters toward the slaves some two centuries ago.

CONCLUSION

I will now bring together the points made above in the form of some concluding observations.

1 The Theory of Plantation Economy is most accurately regarded as part of the tradition of critical analysis of the emergence, spread, and consolidation of world capitalism from its original mercantile

form to its present form of globalized finance capital in crisis. The theory is unique and *sui generis* to the extent that: (1) it employed a unique blend of different approaches, and (2) the specific form of capitalist economy and organization it sought to analyze was itself unique and *sui generis*. The claims to original theorizing are therefore bounded by that historical reality.

2 Hence Plantation Economy theory needs to locate itself within the context of the critical discourse on global capitalism and the existence of non-neoliberal paradigms, including Marxism and neo-Marxism, evolutionary economics, institutional economics, structuralism, and neostructuralism.

3 The model may be strongest in its Pure Plantation Economy version where it represents the situation of island economies in which slave plantations were the dominant unit of production, as in the British and French West Indian islands. Where slave plantations were not as dominant, as in the Hispanic islands, or were part of continental hinterlands, as in Brazil and the U.S. South, the "Pure" model applies to a lesser extents.

4 There is a tension between the elements of continuity and change as Model I evolves into Model II and Model III. The plantation legacy on structures, culture, and patterns of behaviour represents continuity. Change is manifested in new industries, institutions, and ideologies, and in the resistance and survival strategies of the population.

5 The possibility must therefore be conceded that at some point the elements of change may supercede the elements of continuity and make necessary a Kuhn-like paradigm shift. Some would argue that this in fact occurred in the 1980s. This view must be qualified by the consideration that the paradigm shift toward neoliberalism in the 1980s was a global phenomenon. From a Caribbean social sciences perspective, then, it was not a spontaneous development but was imposed from without. There is evidence that by the 1980s the "Plantation Economy school" in the Caribbean was running out of steam, but this may have been due to the absence of innovation based on the original model, absence in part due to the unavailability published material.

6 The absence of an anti-model (Model IV) is a major impediment to appraising the prescriptive value of the theory. It may well be that the specificity of particular plantation societies in politics, social structure, economy, and in relation to the world economy are of equal or greater importance than the plantation legacy in determining appropriate strategies and policies of transformation. Judgment on this question should be suspended pending elaboration of a Model IV.

EPILOGUE

I learned a lot about West Indian history and society from Lloyd [Best], from West Indian students at McGill who formed the core of the Montreal New World Group in the 1960s, and from an intensive reading of West Indian literature. But it was the daily contact with colleagues, co-workers, students, friends, neighbours, and strangers during my years of work in Trinidad, and more recently in Jamaica, which projected me into a continuous learning process which, I suspect, will not end until my final departure. The Caribbean has enriched my life in more ways than I could – or would wish to – tell you.

Those are Kari's words, spoken at the conference to mark the twenty-fifth anniversary of Plantation Economy held at the University of the West Indies, St Augustine, in 1994.

I want to say to Kari that we in the Caribbean are as much in your debt as you have so kindly said you are in ours. I speak of many who are absent on this occasion and others who have passed from this world – like Adlith Brown, who studied here at McGill in the 1960s and who became your close friend and collaborator; like Hugh O'Neale and Alvin Johnson, who organized the McGill Conference on West Indian Affairs in 1967 and who died tragically shortly afterwards; like your friend and comrade in spirit George Beckford, of persistent poverty fame; like Michael Manley, former Prime Minister of Jamaica and Cheddi Jagan, former President of Guyana, both of whom had great admiration for your work; like Willy Demas, former Secretary-General of CARICOM, your close friend and colleague who recently left us.

On behalf of them and hundreds of others who have learned from you over the years I say: We salute you! We big you up! Nuff respec'! and One Love!

NOTES

1 The original essays (Best & Levitt 1969) were bound and circulated in mimeographed form but were never actually published, and hence had only limited availability. Levitt (1998) provides a useful and accessible summary; and Best (1968) provides a detailed exposition of the Pure Plantation Economy model.

2 My own contributions were on the Caribbean bauxite industry and the Caribbean petroleum industry and were contained in volume four of the studies.

3 Through the late 1960s to the end of the 1970s.

4 Notably Guyana, Jamaica, Trinidad and Tobago, and the People's Revolutionary Government (PRG) of Grenada.

REFERENCES

Beckford, George. *Persistent Poverty: Underdevelopment in the Plantation Economies of the Third World.* New York: Oxford University Press, 1972.

Best, Lloyd, and Kari Polanyi Levitt. *Externally Propelled Industrialisation and Growth in the Caribbean: Selected Essays. vols. 1–4.* Montreal: McGill Centre for Developing Area Studies, Unpublished Manuscript, 1969.

Best, Lloyd. "Outline of a Model of Pure Plantation Economy." *Social and Economic Studies,* September 1968.

Girvan, Norman. "Multinational Corporations and Dependent Underdevelopment in Mineral-Export Economies." *Social and Economic Studies,* December 1970.

Levitt, Kari Polanyi. "My collaboration with Lloyd Best." *Marronage* 1 (no. 1, September 1998):1–26.

Levitt, Kari, and Michael Witter, eds. *The Critical Tradition of Caribbean Political Economy: The Legacy of George Beckford.* Kingston: Ian Randle, 1996.

Pantin, Dennis, and Dhanyshar Mahabir, eds. *Plantation Economy Revisited. Marronage* 1 (no. 1, September 1998).

Thomas, Clive Y. *Dependence and Transformation: The Economics of Transition to Socialism.* New York: Monthly Review Press, 1973.

8 The New Canadian Political Economy: Classic and Beyond

MEL WATKINS

It occurred to me as I sat down to write this paper that if my two friends Kari Polanyi Levitt and Gregory Baum are eighty then I must be older than I imagined.

What do an economist and a theologian have in common? Charles Kindleberger, my teacher in graduate school days, liked to tell that he went into his graduate seminar in international economics one year at MIT and there sat a person he had never seen before who was wearing a clerical collar. Kindleberger asked him, "Father, what economics have you taken already?" The priest replied, "That's one branch of theology I haven't studied." Kindleberger claimed he liked his reply so much he let him stay.

We meet in interesting times globally – and under the best of auspices locally. To understand what is happening today in the world economy, you could not do better than to start by reading Karl Polanyi's *The Great Transformation*[1] (and if you have read it, no matter how many times, reread it), just as you should read or reread Kari's *Silent Surrender* as essential background on the prospects for a creative Canadian response.

Political economy is a project in both an intellectual and a political sense, and hence the political economist is – or ought to be – both the scholarly dissenter from orthodoxy and the activist or minimally, the provider of nourishment for the political activist. The great Canadian economic historian Harold Innis wrote of the need for "an economic history of economic history."[2] The symbiotic relationship of political economy with political activism suggests the need for a political economy of political economy, with the discipline presumably keeping pace with the contradictions of capitalism; this enables me to suggest at the outset of this paper that the prospects for political economy presently look good, at least in the sense of good enough.

The combination of scholarship and activism nicely captures the contribution of Polanyi Levitt, notably in her classic book in Canadian political economy, *Silent Surrender.* I was privileged to write the preface to it in 1970 and am therefore in a position to quote myself on this point:

> While Professor Levitt clearly has the skills of the professional economist and uses them here with great effect, she does not play the all-too-common academic game of writing only for her peers and of pretending detachment and neutrality. Rather she writes plainly and forcefully so as to show us the need for alternatives. She is, in the best sense of that term, an intellectual, one who criticizes the *status quo*, and prods us into working out new strategies.[3]

Prior to publication as a book, the longish essay on which *Silent Surrender* was based was published in *New World Quarterly*, then under the editorship of Lloyd Best. The full manuscript had an underground circulation in the late 1960s while awaiting a publisher (it was a Canadian version of the clandestine samizdat in the then USSR); when I told my colleague, the political economist David Wolfe, that I was going to honour Kari in an essay, he said that the manuscript form of *Silent Surrender* – plus a talk by the late Stanley Ryerson – were what radicalized him. Polanyi Levitt was writing at the same time that the Watkins Report (a study on foreign ownership commissioned by the federal government and named after its chief author, the better to disown it) was being written by eight men. None of us at that time, to the cost of the report, was of as radical a persuasion as Kari was.[4]

Others besides myself, like Carleton University's distinguished political economist Wallace Clement, have made the point that Kari's book was a major part of the bridge between the old political economy, as it came to be called, associated with Innis, and the emerging New Canadian Political Economy (NCPE). In fact, it became the most widely used text of the NCPE. The royalties, I like to think, can be counted as one of the few certain benefits of foreign ownership for Canadians – though now that I think about it, Kari probably spent those royalties in the West Indies!

Let me remind you of the opening two sentences of her introduction. "This book presents a sketch of Canada's slide into a position of economic, political and cultural dependence on the United States. It seeks to explain the process whereby national entrepreneurship and political unity have eroded to a point beyond which lies the disintegration of the nation state" (xix). Note in particular the extraordinary prescience of the second sentence. It anticipated a national business class that got its act together so well – notably with the mid-1970s creation of the Business Council on National Issues, now the Canadian Council of Chief Executives, as the shadow government – that it developed the confidence to make a free trade agreement with the United States that further locked in Canada's dependence; it further anticipated a polity that, faced with the clear possibility of splitting in two, tried to solve that problem by fragmenting into ten. If anything Polanyi-Levitt was not pessimistic enough: the Canadian economy was shortly to enter into a sustained period of economic crisis.

In the nature of a bridge, one can, after the event, cross either way. Take Innis's project. We know from John Watson's superb thesis that it was in fact a project both intellectual and political.[5] Innis was not a political activist and denounced 1930s leftists. This is hardly to his credit; still he was what the Innisian scholar Daniel Drache has called an intellectual activist; he believed, truly, that ideas mattered and were not simply something that happened as one walked as briskly as one could, eyes straight ahead – wide shut, as it were – along one's career path.

Innis talked about history as happening through the warp and the woof of time and space; what brings these together is place, a particular part of space rooted in time. Salman Rushdie marvelously captured Innis's Canadian project when he wrote, "In the best writing ... a map of a nation will also turn out to be a map of the world."[6] At a time of "globalization" with its warts now there for all to see, and of the striking multiculturalism of Canada (and elsewhere) that is the opposite side of the coin of globalization and is here to stay, Rushdie's statement is an excellent motto for Canadian political economy.

Innis believed, then, in the need for Canadian theory for the proper study of Canada; it was not sufficient simply to apply theory from outside, meaning the imperial centre, to Canadian problems, as orthodox economists believed then and now. Innis proceeded to create that theory himself as the core of the old political economy paradigm. That Canadian core can be seen as the notion of centre-margin within an imperial system; in that system the margin is staple exporter, and the intellectual in the margin consciously takes advantage of those insights about the centre, about the empire, that are only possible from the margin. Thus it will be evident that Innis was a virtual postmodernist in his understanding of the social construction of knowledge.

Innis's staple approach became the basis for the staple theory, which became another part of the bridge between the old and the new paradigms, on which some people allege I am forever stuck. In a decade like the 1990s, in a world like today's, where one fluctuates between believing that everything has changed and nothing has changed (and the trick is to know which is the case when), it is worth taking a moment to point out the extent to which Canada is apparently still a staples economy and to insist that whatever is done by way of restructuring the paradigm of Canadian political economy, it is essential that truth not be lost.

In the recent currency crises, we were constantly being told that so-called commodity-based economies particularly were in trouble, with commodity prices falling, as they had on trend for twenty-five years. Journalist Bruce Little wrote in the *Globe and Mail* in 1998, "When currency traders around the world think Canada, they think commodities." Former bank economist and now consultant to the private sector, Lloyd Atkinson, was quoted around the same time: "I don't describe this as a dollar crisis. It's a commodity price crisis." They have put their finger on the key reason for the decline of the Canadian dollar from parity with U.S. dollar over that twenty-five year period. World prices for lumber, pulp and paper, copper, iron ore, and nickel have been depressed. The Canadian economy is resource driven and, we are told, that means it is price driven – which was, as it happens, the central theme of the old political economy. Innis is alive and well.

We need to keep in mind that to be a staples producer, to be a "new" country, a settler colony, was to be by definition part of a broader imperial cum global system. Take Innis's *The Cod Fisheries* with its subtitle *The History of an International Economy* to describe the earlier stage of globalization.[7] That will remind us that there are few things new under the imperial sun or, as Polanyi Levitt herself has been heard to say, in effect, "What's new today is less the globalization of markets than the marketing of globalization." Put differently, nothing is so globalized as the rhetoric of globalization and political economists buy into it at a high cost. To read Innis and see how the cyclonics of resource markets impacted on Canada is to be aware both of the long history and the limitations of globalization.

But I must not oversell Innis. For example, while he was aware of the issue of conservation, there is definitely the need, from a contemporary perspective, to explicitly incorporate ecological linkage into staple theorizing. Jamie Linton tells us, "Historically trade has been instrumental in ecosystem degradation and species loss in Canada ... the ecological terms of trade are stacked against the staple exporter from the beginning." He cites Innis's contemporary and collaborator, A.R.M. Lower: "A staple trade is in essence a mining operation. It takes nature's bounties as it finds them, and it leaves a desert behind." The case for fleshing out that insight in all its fullness is clear.[8]

Crossing the bridge the other way, we come to the NCPE with its focus on foreign ownership, which the old paradigm had neglected as part of its larger neglect of industrial development. The issue had been in the air politically from the 1950s, with John Diefenbaker,[9] Walter Gordon, and the left nationalist wing of the Liberal Party. Then came the Watkins Report in the 1960s, and as the decade closed the Waffle group as a left nationalist caucus within the New Democratic Party. It all culminated in Kari's *Silent Surrender.* Canada came to be understood as being a branch-plant economy, a dependent economy with an underdeveloped industrial sector. Levitt famously described Canada as having "a rich, industrialized, underdeveloped economy"; this became shortened in the telling to Canada as "the richest underdeveloped country," a phrase that so nicely captured the spirit of Canadian nationalism in the 1960s. Levitt's focus, like that of the Watkins Report – here I was much influenced by Abraham Rotstein and the late Stephen Hymer – was less on foreign ownership *per se*, and more on the multinational corporation as a threat to the sovereignty, the very being, of the nation-state itself. These ideas entered the Canadian political discourse.

The basis was laid for the grand neo-Innisian synthesis: the Naylor-Clement thesis, with further embellishments by Glen Williams and Gordon Laxer. Along the way, the spirit of it was captured in Riane Mahon's phrase, "the staples fraction," to describe the dominant fraction of the Canadian capitalist class. This Canadian marriage of Innis and Marx lay at the core of the NCPE.[10] David Langille's classic article on the then Business Council on National Issies caps the NCPE; it begins the shift in political discourse, since then so notable among activists, to corporate rule, as in Tony Clarke's *Silent Coup: Confronting the Big Business Takeover of Canada.*[11] (That repetition of "Silent" suggests the time has come for us to become a noisier people as, indeed, we seem to have become in our opposition to the Multilateral Agreement on Investment – and then the Free Trade Area of the Americas.)

At the same time, Polanyi Levitt was taking a most enlightened position on Quebec; the French-language edition of *Silent Surrender* had a preface by Jacques Parizeau – who went on to later infamy. The English-Canadian nationalist movement was sufficiently large to imagine that it could afford a split on Quebec, with Levitt and the NCPE (and the Waffle), supportive of Quebec nationalism. Come the late 1980s, the support of Quebec nationalists for free trade, in sharp contrast with the opposition of English-Canadian left nationalists, explains why almost no one in English Canada now supports Quebec's national project.

The NCPE was, and is, much broader than its economics core. We need only to remember that this New Left political economy came out of the 1960s, the last great decade; if you missed it, put it down to bad timing on your part. Hence its broad concerns with class, nation (including internal nations), gender, and race – otherwise known as life. Clement's *Understanding Canada* lists no fewer than eighteen topics that merit their own chapter. The writings, notably of the philosopher Charles Taylor, on identities have come to inform the new paradigm.[12] At the same time, "identities" became unambiguously the new core of Canadian Studies which was closely linked as a project to NCPE, and which Innis and Grant had also initially influenced.

The profound change in university curricula since the 1960s owes something to the NCPE. Witness the fluorescence of Canadian Studies, Aboriginal or Native Studies, Women's Studies, Gay and Lesbian Studies, plus Environmental Studies, Cultural Studies, and Peace and Conflict Studies. (The motto seems to be: If it moves, study it.) The academic triumph of political economy is everywhere impressive *except*, and this matters, and not just to Kari and me as economists, in economics (a point to which I shall return).

I had the good fortune once to hear the American economist Kenneth Boulding lay out the criteria for a paradigm based on his own pioneering work in Peace and Conflict Studies: you must be able to teach courses in it; give a degree in it; compile a bibliography; write a text book; have a refereed learned journal and a professional association. By all these criteria, NCPE is a paradigm in its own right. Of course to be so "institutionalized" is problematic, as the New Left, to say nothing of Max Weber, should have taught us. The success of NCPE in the academy risks the loss of its political edge.

What then of the effects of the NCPE outside the academy? The philosopher and cultural theorist Ian Angus, in his recent book *A Border Within*, writes of the left nationalist school: "The account of economic dependence was thoroughly documented, but did not have significant impact on Canadian society or policy."[13] That seems true enough in a literal and direct sense, economic dependence having arguably increased rather than decreased, but there may be significant consequences all the same.

Like the extraordinary change in the Canadian labour movement from mostly "international" to mostly national (pushed by the Waffle-inspired stream of the NCPE) and with autonomy bordering on independence for the Quebec labour movement. The Canadian Auto Workers and public sector unions in particular were the basis for the concerted opposition of the labour movement to the Free Trade Agreement and NAFTA, and for new-style, militant, left nationalist politics. The CAW, with its concern with international solidarity, notably with Mexican workers, can be seen as exemplary. This nationalist shift is quite stunning when contrasted with the fullness of the embrace of continentalism by the Canadian business class; if a Canada with a social democratic cast survives, this change in the labour movement may well be the decisive reason.

And the articulation of the Canadian welfare state, the sleeper issue of the great free trade debate of the late 1980s. It is here, particularly in health care, that Canadians differentiate themselves from Americans. Surely the legitimizing of that sense of Canada as a distinct society in need of greater distinction was at the core of the NCPE, while the scholarly work on Swedish social democracy, notably by Carleton University political economists, has been a direct impetus.[14]

The major problem with the NCPE is that it is rather long in the tooth; it no longer seems all that new as everywhere the ground shifts under our feet. Angus argues the FTA was the death of left nationalism: "Globalization has finished the English-Canadian left-nationalist politics" (ix). As we approached – and passed – the tenth anniversary of the FTA, there is a need to recognize that it has affected everything, including our ability to think; we on the left seem at times to have lost that essential sense of place, the ground on which to stand.

With the FTA came further large increases in cross-border trade and investment between Canada and the United States, and a further giant slither of the Canadian economy into the American economy. The export-led model in resources has been supplemented by the export-led model in manufacturing. The Asian economic crisis of the late 1990s cast considerable doubt on the export-led model in general. Increases in exports of Canadian manufactures are much touted by business and pro-business commentators but, of course, are offset by imports.

Interestingly, Canadian productivity seems for the longest time not to have increased in the manner proponents of free trade predicted, with Canadian competitiveness apparently being maintained by the depreciating dollar. *The Globe and Mail*'s 16 October 1998 Report on Business had a story about a report by the Conference Board of Canada, a "respectable" (meaning pro-business) body, on how Canada's poor productivity performance explained why the Canadian standard of living was falling relative to other countries, including the United States:

> James Frank, the board's chief economist, said the slow growth of Canadian productivity has been one of the major surprises of the 1990s. Free trade with the United States gave Canadian companies access to larger markets and allowed them to rationalize their production, he said. "That in theory should

have led to more rapid growth in productivity in the smaller economy. That is happening [actually, the point of the story is that it isn't], but much less quickly than we had (anticipated)," he said. Canadian companies have invested heavily in new machinery and Canadian workers are well trained and educated, but management may not have been aggressive enough to take advantage of the broader North American market, Mr. Frank said ... "It takes longer to get that entrepreneurship going than I would have expected."

If Mr Frank had read the NCPE, which provided the intellectual support for the opposition to the FTA, he would not have been surprised; the point was made not only that the "theory" to which he alludes was deeply flawed but that a Royal Commission on agricultural machinery discovered in the 1960s that the Canadian industry remained significantly less productive than its American counterpart in spite of some two decades of free trade. In the market test of who best predicted the effects of free trade on Canada, the NCPE outperformed orthodox economics; that, it seems to me, is a matter well worth noting. It is likewise evident that we need an up-to-date political economy study of the Canadian business class in the era of free trade; just how continentalist is it in its structure and orientation, in its values and behaviour?

There is much to be learned from Angus's rich analysis: on how "dependency" prepared the mind for thinking about domination in general,[15] on "border" as the leading metaphor with which Canadians can counter globalization; on the symbiosis between globalization and identities; and on new social movements with transnational linkages – to which political economy is linked and with which it has to develop a counter-political discourse. The Mexican intellectual Adolpho Guilly makes the powerful point that at the heart of a political discourse that runs counter to the dominant discourse of globalization centred on corporate rights must be the issue of human rights.

Paradoxically, at the margin there must continue to be a "nationalist" component – if not an explicit nationalist discourse, then a discourse about nationalism and serious academic work thereon. The neglect of the proper study of nationalism remains the great blind spot of political economists of all persuasions in many parts of the world; indeed, this is an area in which Canadian political economy could make a contribution to global as well as Canadian studies. There are encouraging signs. Gordon Laxer has taken on the large project of exploring the relationship between globalization and nationalism: "Of central concern ... is the new right's effective use of global and populist appeals to sell the efficacy of pure capitalism and the economic benefits of inequality. This challenge reintroduces the national question onto centre stage, a position it has not held in most advanced capitalist countries since the Second World War."[16]

Faced with globalization the harder left in Canada has, albeit belatedly, become nationalist![17] There has been and must continue to be a central concern with the internal nations of Canada and collective rights of the aboriginal peoples and the Québecois.

More generally, social democratic guru Anthony Giddens writes in his *The Third Way: The Renewal of Social Democracy*: "The nation-state is not disappearing, and the scope of government, taken overall, expands rather than diminishes as globalization proceeds."[18] Globalization creates chaos and a host of problems old and new that require a more active nation-state: we need health-care, more of it; we need education, more of it in a so-called knowledge economy.[19]

Both Kari Polanyi Levitt and I being economists, perhaps I can be allowed to make a special plea, to bring economics, in the sense of the study of the state of the economy, more clearly into political economy. This is necessary in order to counter the discourse of neoconservatism, to restore some balance in a postmodern world where the discourse of politics is overwhelmingly materialist (a.k.a. greedy) and the intellectual discourse of postmodernism studiously ignores the economy in any substantive sense.

As globalization shows its dark side, the rhetoric of neoconservatism, which is so destructive of community and of the concerns of political economy, increasingly rings hollow. Keynes wrote of capitalism in the 1930s: "It is not beautiful, it is not just, it is not virtuous – and it doesn't deliver the goods."[20] For a while after World War II, with the help of Keynesianism, capitalism did deliver the goods to enough of the people enough of the time, but growing inequalities nationally and globally show it is no longer doing that.

At a time when the centre of politics has shifted well to the right and capitalism is hegemonic, there is, I think, a need for the academic left in Canada to take social democratic politics, intellectually and practically, more seriously, to be involved in its renewal. Much could be learned from Polanyi on limits to commodification and limits to markets that could inform the discourse of social democracy.

In the moral crisis of the 1960s, the essence of the NCPE manifested itself in the struggles within the NDP between the left and the mainstream; the further left, the Waffle, lost, which, given what we now know about the nature of social democracy, should sadden but not surprise us. But since then the labour movement, which was to the right of the Party has moved to its left, social movements have proliferated, and the new leader of the NDP, Jack Layton, has healed old divisions and put all this together. The times seem propitious to have a sustained dialogue between the NDP and political economists. Perhaps there should be a third edition of *Social Planning/Purpose for Canada*.[21]

Finally, has the time now come for Canadian scholars, on the margin, to study the United States, the centre? The absence of such research is striking, though there is the later Innis on the history of the press in the U.S. and others, like Marshall McLuhan, George Grant, and Ursula Franklin, have written indirectly about the U.S. via their studies of technology, which is so American-centred in this century. Significantly, James Laxer, who has a keen sense of the cutting issues, has done a book on the Americans.[22] The time has come for us to study the Americans in the hope that it will benefit us – and, yet less certainly, them.

NOTES

1 Karl Polanyi, *The Great Transformation* (Boston: Beacon, 1944); Kari Levitt, *Silent Surrender: the Multinational Corporation in Canada* (Toronto: Macmillan, 1970), and the recently published second edition.

2 Harold Innis, "On the Economic Significance of Cultural Factors" in *Political Economy in the Modern State* (Toronto: Ryerson, 1946):83.

3 Kari Levitt, *Silent Surrender: The Multinational Corporation in Canada* (Toronto: Macmillan of Canada, 1971):ix. Mel Watkins also has written the Preface to the new edition of *Silent Surrender: The Multinational Corporation in Canada* (Montreal: McGill-Queen's University Press, 2002) [Editor's note].

4 Canada, *Foreign Ownership and the Structure of Canadian Industry: Report of the Task Force on the Structure of Canadian Industry* (Ottawa: Privy Council Office, 1968).

5 Alexander John Watson, *Marginal Man: Harold Innis' Communications Works in Context* Doctoral dissertation, University of Toronto, 1981; a revised version will be published shortly by the University of Toronto Press.

6 Salman Rushdie in *Harper's*, 1997 (September).

7 Harold Innis, *The Cod Fisheries: The History of an International Economy*. Rev. ed. (Toronto: University of Toronto Press, 1954).

8 Jamie Linton, "An Ecological History of Canadian Exports." *Innis Research Bulletin*. A publication of the Harold Innis Research Institute. Issue 2, 1994 (November).

9 Diefenbaker failure to deliver on the new Canadianism he inspired resulted in George Grant's *Lament for a Nation*. See George Grant, *Lament for a Nation: The Defeat of Canadian Nationalism* (Toronto: McClelland & Stewart, 1965).

10 See Mel Watkins, "Canadian Capitalism in Transition" in *Understanding Canada: Building on the New Canadian Political Economy*, ed. Wallace Clement (Montreal and Kingston: McGill-Queen's University Press, 1997):19–42.

11 Langille, "The Business Council on National Issues and the Canadian State," *Studies in Political Economy* 24, 1987 (autumn); Tony Clarke, *Silent Coup: Confronting the Big Business Takeover of Canada* (Toronto: Lorimer, 1997).

12 See in particular his "Shared and Divergent Values" in *Options for a New Canada*, ed. Ron Watts and Douglas Brown (Toronto: University of Toronto Press, 1991).

13 Angus, *A Border Within: National Identity, Cultural Plurality, and Wilderness* (Montreal and Kingston: McGill-University Press. 1997):35. *A Border Within* is an excellent and thought-provoking book; this essay could be seen as an extended commentary on it.

14 On the latter, see in particular, Wallace Clement and Rianne Mahon eds., *Swedish Social Democracy: A Model in Transition* (Toronto: Canadian Scholars' Press, 1994).

15 See the prescient A. Kontos ed., *Domination* (Toronto: University of Toronto Press, 1975).

16 Gordon Laxer, "Nationalism, the Left and Globalization." Paper presented to the Canadian Political Science Association, Charlottetown, May 1992:10.

17 See recent issues of *The Socialist Register.*

18 Anthony Giddens, *The Third Way: The Renewal of Social Democracy* (Cambridge: Polity Press, 1998).

19 Still, the international economy is increasingly evolving into a global economy where capital is sovereign, albeit with a hierarchy of "national" capitals; Canadian capital has to be situated within that context. Resistance increasingly manifests itself in globally linked NGOs which oppose corporate globalization in the name of democracy. See Michael Hardt and Antônio Negri, *Empire* (Cambridge: Harvard University Press, 2000). That political economy can thrive in Canada under these circumstances is evident in the world-wide sales of Naomi Klein's most creative *No Logo: Taking Aim at the Brand Bullie* (Toronto: Knopf Canada, 2000).

20 John Maynard Keynes, "National Self-Sufficiency." *The Yale Review* 22(4), 1933 (June), 772.

21 League for Social Reconstruction, *Social Planning for Canada* (Toronto: University of Toronto Press, 1975 [1935]); Michael Oliver, ed., *Social Purpose for Canada* (Toronto: University of Toronto Press, 1961).

22 James Laxer, *Stalking the Elephant: My Discovery of America* (Toronto: Viking, 2000).

9 Kari Polanyi Levitt and Critical Thought in the Caribbean: A Sketch

MICHAEL WITTER

In 1973, when I was helping my Ph.D. advisor to reorganize his office at Stanford University, I noticed a set of bound manuscripts in the dustbin. They turned out to be copies of the original papers setting out various models of "Plantation Economy" written by Kari and Lloyd Best. These fascinating documents were to inspire my doctoral thesis on the growth of export economies in which I focused on the accumulation process that underpinned the dependency of the export economy. Shortly after my thesis was submitted, I discovered that Samir Amin had already covered much of what I had written in his "centre-periphery" model of accumulation.

In many ways I could present a variation of much the same material Lloyd Best and Norman Girvan present, our differences here and there might help to further illuminate the profound impact that Kari Polanyi Levitt has had on Caribbean economic thought. Instead, I will try to bring back the discussion to a complex central theme of Kari's work, particularly with Lloyd Best, Norman Girvan, and George Beckford: that democracy has to go beyond multi-party elections to the level of economic decision making so as to release the creativity, and especially the entrepreneurship, of the people for social and economic development. Parenthetically, Norman suggested and I concur, that in many parts of the Caribbean today – Jamaica and Guyana, for example – the survival of the society ought to be of more concern than development. Given that Russian society has recently fallen apart, societal disintegration is not a far-fetched possibility.

Jamaica, you see, has been structurally adjusted and stabilized more than any other society in the world. Norman told you that Jamaica's economic performance has been dismal under structural adjustment, and he alluded to a profound opening of the historical race and class splits in the society. The youth are tied in to an international culture in a way that makes them extremely vulnerable in a society which imports over 90 per cent of its protein. They want to eat cornflakes, wear Nike shoes, and play computer games. The young men wear earrings, with their brand name pants dropping off their bottoms.

We have been living with what the Asians are now experiencing for twenty-five years. It has made us weaker and less able to cope with the changes in the international economy today. The Jamaican government spends about 65 per cent of its revenue on debt payments. Conceive of that! Therefore, it has to go out and borrow money in today's world. Even if it can get loans, how can the government repay them? Our earnings are likely to fall tremendously as the prices of our exports fall; and as our North American visitors husband their incomes more, so will our tourist earnings fall.

If you were able to fly over and look down through the roofs of the houses into Jamaican society, you would see a state of civil war. Once upon a time, when anything went wrong, we wrote petitions, we held meetings, and we expressed collective positions. To me the most important cost of this structural adjustment has been the promotion of rank individualism: people no longer get together to try to sort out their common difficulties but act on their own vis-à-vis those over whom they have power. That explains why over 60 per cent of the murders in Jamaica are among family and friends and within neighbourhoods. This is a society that is not exploding as much as it is imploding. The individualism where each person seeks his or her own solution to the problems of survival has inevitably broken down the fundamental institutions in the society, starting with the family, the neighbourhood community, and any form of collective activity.

I agree that the policies of liberalism, and their underlying rationale, came in with the World Bank and the International Monetary Fund. In our case, they came at a time when radical thought was influential, though I do not think dominant, within the university and the wider community of scholars, certainly within my Department of Economics. Today, our department has a strong core of young neoliberals of the most conservative type. Some of them are my students, by the way, and I worked hard to get them into North American universities. But they came back enamoured by mathematical models, intolerant of any kind of discourse critiquing neoclassical economics, and committed to the Washington consensus.

Over the last two decades, Kari has spent a lot of time with us teaching and doing research. She has worked in the face of hostility from the neoliberals and without much support from many of the former progressive thinkers who were demoralized and scattered to the winds, as it were, in the changed political circumstances. Kari stood up, not offering dogma, but inviting us to think, to be critical, to pay attention to issues from the agenda of neoliberal discourse.

Today, Joseph Stiglitz from the World Bank tells us, "You know that beneath these deteriorating economic indicators, there are people!"; that the institutional destruction brought on by this one-size-fits-all prescription has exacerbated, not corrected, the current crisis in Russia and Asia; that the rapid liberalization of these economies without regulatory frameworks explains some of their vulnerability to sudden reversals of the movement of short-term capital. Stiglitz talks about "Voice"; that people, especially those affected negatively by neoliberal policies, are not being consulted; that the long-term effects of cutting public expenditure on social services are likely to inhibit the economy's capacity to grow and develop.[1]

In Jamaica, illiteracy is growing. Men are twice as likely to be illiterate as women, yet women are more than twice as likely to be malnourished as babies than men. There has been a devastation of what many call social capital: the savaging of human resources and the relations between people necessary for any kind of social process. It is Kari who keeps reminding us that the unequal distribution of income in our society is undermining our capacity to grow. Never mind this notion that national savings will increase if income is shifted from the poor to the rich, because the rich save at a higher rate. Kari knew that, for a variety of historical reasons, our rich people tend to consume more, rather than save more, when they get a higher share of the national income. Even Jeffrey Sachs from Harvard and Martin Feldstein from the National Bureau of Research of the U.S.A. are now critiquing the appropriateness of the IMF forcing institutional/structural reform on the Asian countries.

In a sense the radical critique, to which Kari contributed so much, has been vindicated. We have listened to Kari over the years in classrooms, in public lectures, in research seminars, in informal discussions with her colleagues, and on radio talk shows make these arguments over and over. But in another sense, it is very sad that so much destruction of our humanity and society has taken place before someone like Joseph Stiglitz from the World Bank could make the profound observation that there are people down there, somewhere.

I do not worry so much about the actual debt; I gave you an index of its enormity in Jamaica. I really worry about what it has done to us as a people. We seem to have lost our confidence in our capacity to transform our reality, and I question how capable our society is of surviving. Norman alluded to the breakdown in Jamaican society. In Jamaica, there is not really much difference among the three major political parties in their embrace of liberal economic policies. The government consults their international advisors but ignores the people, except at elections. As a result, some communities have created alternate structures and institutions around informal economic activities, with their alternate system of justice. We may not approve of the dominant morality in these communities that condones trade in illegal drugs and guns, extorts the business classes, and smuggles one thing or another. But the informal economy is a survival mechanism for the people.

In recent years, there has been an increasing frequency of spontaneous demonstrations, such as blocking of roads, to protest the lack of water and other utilities, poor road and transport facilities, unfair competition from imports, and every form of high-handed and corrupt behaviour by public officials, particularly the police. When major roads are blocked, everything stops, and the government must deal with the issue at hand. The police recently went into a community to arrest a man, whom the people regard as their leader. Kingston was shut down for three days in a one-on-one confrontation between women, children, and unemployed men on the one side, and the police force with their armoured vehicles and their big guns on the other side. The police had to bring out this community leader, who by their definition was a notorious criminal wanted for murder, to address his angry supporters with a megaphone so as to calm them.

When the press asked some of the demonstrators what they wanted, they complained about injustice, about the way they were constantly disrespected by the police and other public authorities, about having no voice. To me, that kind of spontaneous manifestation was the way in which those people were claiming their democracy. This is very thin political ice because it leaves the way open for someone who sees the need for law and good order.

I think the notion of reclaiming democracy is very important. Today the Caribbean is more dominated by transnational corporations, including international financial institutions, than ever before. The struggles of the Caribbean people must be linked to the struggles of the people who live in the advanced country where strategic decisions about the transnational operations are made. Parenthetically, standing on Rue Ste Catherine, it seems to me that Montreal has had some similar negative economic impact over the past ten years. Sidewalks are crumbling, and it is clear that there are many more poor people now, officially estimated at 40 per cent. My colleagues here tell me that we at the University of the West Indies are not the only people with graduate students who are semi-literate. It is an international phenomenon.

I think that until our state and our society gets a little space from the dominance of the international lending institutions in the form of debt relief or whatever, it will not be possible to address the question of democracy at the level of the economy. Whether we get the space or not, policy makers need guidance from critical thinkers in a rapidly changing world. We may interpret these mass manifestations as cries for democracy. But we must devise new strategies for development appropriate to our historical conditions and the likely future of the world economy if we are to go beyond cries for democracy to deepen democracy in Jamaica.

NOTE

1 Joseph Stiglitz has left the World Bank. He received the Nobel Peace Prize in Economics in 2001 and is currently professor of economics and finance, Columbia University.

10 Reconciling the Transition to Socialism

SAMIR AMIN

This discussion of the transition from capitalism to socialism begins with a deceptively simple statement.[1] Conceptions of the transition depend on what is meant by capitalism and socialism. Major currents of the historical left have never agreed on the essential nature of capitalism – or of its antithesis, socialism. Disagreements also exist within Marxism. Strategies of transcending capitalism – whether democracy in the west, bolshevism, Maoism, or radical anti-imperialism in the Third World, to mention only the most important – differ significantly from each other.

A second observation is equally simple: history has failed to prove the validity of any of these theories. Rather it has demonstrated their shortcomings, as illustrated by the erosion of the welfare state, the collapse of the Soviet systems, the abandonment of Maoism in China, and the compradorization of the Third World. Moreover, capitalism evolves and transforms as history advances. The various definitions of capitalism may need to be revised to take into account significant qualitative changes, such as the new "globalization."

THE CAPITALIST MODE OF PRODUCTION AND REALLY EXISTING WORLD CAPITALISM: THREE FUNDAMENTAL CONTRADICTIONS OF THE SYSTEM

I suggest that the capitalist system is defined by three fundamental contradictions. These are essential in the sense that the system is incapable of even conceptualizing their resolution. I then consider to what measure different historical currents of socialism and Marxism have shared the conceptions outlined here. This paper will prepare the ground for an evaluation of different approaches to the transition to socialism, in theory and practice.

The three fundamental characteristics of capitalism are:

1 Relations of production which define the specific form of alienation of the worker and the economic laws of capitalism.
2 Polarization on a global scale, unprecedented in all of human history.
3 Inability to halt the degradation of the natural environment on a scale which threatens the future of the human race.

Economic Alienation

The first of these characteristics is shared by all currents of Marxism, because it constitutes the essential definition of the capitalist mode of production. From this common point of departure, however, many divergences reveal themselves as soon as we proceed to specific relations of production, the law of value, the relationship between class conflict and economic laws, between the economic base and the ideological superstructure, etc. Divergences are even greater when we consider the entire anti-capitalist left, in all its manifestations. A recapitulation of the following propositions serves to illustrate this observation.

1 Capitalist relations of production do not assume their final form until the advent of the industrial revolution. In industrial capitalism, private ownership of the means of production whereby wage labour is exploited, is largely dissociated from previous forms of control over access to natural resources (land) because the means of production (the factories) are themselves the product of labour. The period which precedes this qualitative leap in the development of the forces of production (which we date at about 1800) can be read, in retrospect, as the (mercantilist) transition to capitalism.
2 These capitalist relations of production constitute the framework within which value and the "law of value" operates. Society appears to organize itself into a series of closed markets integrated into a three-dimensional generalized system of markets for products, labour, and capital.
3 These markets appear to function "autonomously." The dynamic which drives them appears to obey laws independent of human will analogous to the operation of the laws of nature. These "economic

laws" become objective forces. Economic alienation is a new phenomenon, a historical product of the emergence of full-scale capitalism. In previous societies there were no objective laws which controlled social reproduction. Economic alienation is a characteristic of the modern world; it contrasts with the metaphysical alienation of earlier tributary class society. In capitalism, the law of value controls more than the reproduction of the economic system; it controls all aspects of social life.

4 The alienation of the worker is set in this framework, as an expression of the exigencies of economic alienation in the domain of "labour markets." The sellers of labour power must live in an existential state of submission to objective laws over which they have no control.

5 The relations among the economic base (the economy), the political management of society (the state), and the ideologies whereby social forces express themselves are similarly constrained within this framework. Capitalism is a system which separates the organization of political life from the economy, which functions by itself. This separation is also a historical innovation. Previous tributary systems were defined by the subordination of the economic to the political sphere: I have described this reversal by stating that in tributary systems "power controls wealth"; but in capitalism "wealth controls power." Economic alienation (of labour) thus replaces metaphysical alienation (the dominance of ideologies which permit the reproduction of power). The separation of politics from economics is fundamental to the formation of modern political systems, including bourgeois democracy.

This brief exposé illustrates the extent of divergences concerning the essential question, "What is capitalism?" Whereas I place emphasis on the qualitative rupture which distinguishes capitalism from all previous systems, an opposing view proceeds from a general definition of characteristics common to all societies (the economic base, the relations of production, the state, classes and the political level, the ideological superstructure), and analyzes the mechanisms of the articulation of these characteristics in the same manner in all societies. For example, the economic base is always subject to objective laws; it always controls the movement of history; the superstructure always reflects the requirements of the reproduction of the economic base, etc. This view diminishes the importance of economistic alienation, including alienation of labour, in my account of capitalism.

As I am not inclined to accept the usefulness of a papacy charged with delivering certificates of Marxist authenticity – indeed I see it as a danger – I will not discuss these different theses within the terrain of Marxology. I simply observe, and will later elaborate, that concepts which are significantly different from the five points of my brief account were – and remain – dominant in the anti-capitalist left, not only within Marxism of the Third International (certainly in Soviet although not necessarily in Maoist currents) but also in the two other principal "antisystemic" forces, western social democracy and the radical populist anti-imperialism of the peripheries.

But our conceptions of capitalism largely define our vision of the superior classless society, which is or should be the object of our struggles. These conceptions exercise a decisive influence on the strategies of transition we might develop to bring us closer to socialism, if that is the name we give to the objective of our struggles. The object of my critique is the reduction of socialism to a vulgar "capitalism without capitalists." We will see that, notwithstanding important differences and divergences, all the strategies of transition to socialism proposed in the past shared common elements which derive from conceptions concerning the nature of capitalism and socialism. This is true of gradualistic social democracy since Bernstein; revolutionary social democracy and later Trotskyism; the construction of socialism according to the Third International; revolution by Maoist stages; market socialism of worker-controlled syndicalism, whether Marxist, anarchist, socialist or whatever; Titoism; post-Maoist China; or various Third-World versions of a "non-capitalist road."

Global Polarization

When we consider the second characteristic of capitalism, disagreements are even more marked. Never in the history of humanity have inequalities in the development of productive forces, that is, in the productivity of social labour, been so extreme as they have become in the era of capitalism. In 1800 differences in per capita production rarely surpassed levels of 1 to 2; today the gap between developed capitalist countries and societies emerging from the initial stages of development are at levels of 1 to 50. Moreover, whereas the dominant tendency of long-term development in pre-capitalist times was one of "catching up" (backward Europe was able to catch up with more developed Asia between 1000 and 1500 CE), capitalism has aggravated trends of polarization. It is paradoxical that the dominant ideological discourse of "globalization" holds out the promise of accelerated progress by the modernization of backward societies.

Given the scale of these phenomena, social thought is remarkably unconvincing. Its dominant currents maintain two parallel – and contrary – discourses, without shame or embarrassment. On the one hand, we have the discourse of conventional economics, where it is claimed that capitalist globalization offers everybody the opportunities to development. On the other hand, there is need to explain why these opportunities have not been exploited; why divergences in income and wealth are even more extreme. In the parallel discourse which seeks to respond to this challenge, economics is totally absent: the argument turns on differences of culture, religions or ethnicity – called "race" before that term became politically incorrect because of excesses committed in its name.

By contrast, anti-capitalist currents of thought could well have exploited the scandal of global polarization which has accompanied the expansion of capitalism. To this end, attention could and should have been accomplished by focusing on the relation between polarization and capitalism to develop a theory of that relationship. This, broadly speaking, has not been done. Proponents may believe that they have addressed these problems, but this has been in a manner and with arguments which appear highly debatable.

Fortunately, social thought and science will always remain incomplete, and historical materialism is no exception. Concerning the central question of social evolution, historical materialism has given rise to divergent theses: some emphasize laws of general validity for all societies; others by contrast, point out specific peculiarities to explain specific outcomes. The explanation of these divergences lies in the fact that we lack a satisfactory theory of the articulation of the economic, political, and cultural aspects of society. Whereas Marxism has produced a coherent and holistic theory of capitalist production, it has not succeeded in developing equally convincing analyses of power and of culture. One trend in Marxism treats the articulation of the economic, political, and cultural levels of society in a manner which produces a universal history (the "five stages" of primitive communism: slavery, feudalism, capitalism, and socialism – certainly a caricature!), while the other explains backwardness and development impasses and blockages with theories such as the Asiatic mode of production. Both of these trends claim to be true to the essential tenets of Marxism. For my part, I proposed to bypass this conflict between two eurocentric schools by theorizing social evolution in terms of three stages: the communal, the tributary, and the capitalist.

It will hardly be surprising that important differences reveal themselves when we address the immediate issue of polarization in modern times. As far as I am concerned, the dominant tendency has always underestimated – to say the least! – the importance of the phenomenon of polarization. But why?

To find the answer we must re-examine the philosophy of the Enlightenment, the constitution of the ideology of modern (bourgeois) rationalism, and that of the working-class and socialist movements, Marxism included. This is a history of powerful expressions of optimism, leading to the triumph of reason, and thus of progress, that is, the progressive dissolution of backwardness: quite the contrary of polarization. This is where bourgeois thought has remained, its economism finding naïve expression in "theories of economic development" which assume that if "correct" choices are made, the rest – politics and culture – will automatically adjust, or be adjusted.

But Marx, and socialists of the era, fully shared this optimism. Did Marx not affirm that the law of value, once released from Pandora's box, would become an irresistible force sweeping away all resistance to progress? Neither nations nor states, ideologies nor politicians, not even religions could resist its effects, both devastating (destruction of peasantry and crafts; reduction of all popular classes to sellers of labour power) and liberating (forces of production and individuals). Unequal development, polarization, growing disparities were thus no more than transient accidents. The dominant tendency of capitalist expansion was the formation, sooner or later, of one integrated society on a world scale, founded on the single social contradiction which opposes the bourgeoisie to the proletariat. According to this view, capitalism would prepare its demise by socialist revolution on a world scale. In the meantime, the history of capitalism would entail the subordination of all aspects of social life to the unilateral needs of its economic existence. Does this not sound like the neoliberal defense of the market economy?

If this reading of Marx sounds like a caricature, it is in my view, no more so than that which both the Second and Third International imposed on historical Marxism. Corrections were made to take into account the inescapable fact of growing international polarization – but without calling into question the fundamental theory whereby the laws of accumulation of capital would eventually result in its demise. The most important of these corrections was Lenin's theory of imperialism, which attributed polarization to the (relatively) recent transformation of (competitive) capitalism into monopoly capitalism since approximately 1880.

The challenges to these dogmas by the reverse hypothesis, that is, that polarization is not due to political or cultural resistance to capitalism resulting from its expansion, is a recent development. It constitutes the leitmotif of my research since its beginning in the 1950s, and that of the so-called dependency schools of Latin America and world systems theory. While similarities and divergences within these schools have received sufficient attention to warrant no further discussion here, it is necessary to note that we are dealing not with abstract theoretical conceptualizations but with ideas which have provided historical social movements with an ideological framework.

Because the implicit response to polarization has played a decisive role in ideas about revolution and the construction of socialism, we cannot counterpose different and new concepts regarding the transition to socialism to historically outmoded and bankrupt ones without summarizing the theory of polarization. I will limit myself to conclusions I have arrived at without reference to their genesis or their relation to the above-mentioned schools.

I maintain that polarization is the result of the operation of the law of value on a world scale. This implies the recognition of the dominance of the economic sphere, peculiar to capitalism compared with all previous systems. This dominance forms the first distinguishing characteristic of capitalism noted above.

Although historical Marxism shared this thesis, it was (falsely) believed that homogenizing forces would prevail over polarizing ones. In explanations of the (inescapable) reality of polarization, Marxism abandoned the primacy of economic factors in favour of explanations in terms of political and cultural resistances to capitalist expansion. Where did historical Marxism go wrong?

The Marxist error lies in confusing the law of value in a general and abstract form, which defines capitalism as a "mode of production," with the law of value on a world scale, manifested in the global expansion of really existing capitalism. While the former implies the general integration of a global market, the latter is a truncated world market which excludes labour. Historical Marxism has conflated the world expansion of capitalism with the expansion of the capitalist mode of production, which should be distinguished. We maintain that it is uniquely the operation of the law of value which results in polarization, and that polarization has been immanent in capitalism since its earliest forms. Polarization is not a recent phenomenon corresponding to a stage of imperialism; nor is it due to political or cultural resistance to capitalism. The law of value on a world scale explains the specific characteristics of peripheral capitalism: the disintegration of productive systems (compared with integrated autocentric capitalism); dependence; the reproduction of pre-capitalist modes of production, deformed and subordinated to the logic of capitalist accumulation (in opposition to the destruction of pre-capitalist formations in central countries); and the deformations of "modern" political systems in peripheral states. Political and cultural resistance, far from being vestiges of the past, are reactions to the challenges of polarizing capitalism.

However, the ideas developed here are no more than ideas. Anti-capitalist movements are unaware of them. The "transition" clings to false theories and pragmatic adjustments. According to these theories, capitalist expansion prepares the conditions for a world socialist revolution. Or at the very least, if all the world's peoples have not yet reached the level of the most advanced centres when the bell tolls the arrival of the revolution, the peripheries will be pulled along and enabled to catch up to the more advanced countries at an accelerated rate. Revolution in the centres appears as second best to world revolution. Is this not reminiscent of Lenin's expectations that revolution in Europe would come to his help after the Russian Revolution was launched at the weakest link in the capitalist chain? Nor was the social democratic vision, whereby accumulation in the centres would eventually lead to socialism pulling along the peripheries, essentially different.

But the attack on the capitalist order did not follow this theoretical schema. Rather revolutions began in the outer regions – and remained locked in there. An accommodation to these realities produced a legitimation of a theory of the construction of socialism in one country. Launched under the label of Leninism, this line of thought was developed by Mao as a theory of permanent revolution by stages, with evident debt to Trotsky and even to Lenin. It was even believed possible to stretch the legitimacy of this version of the transition to socialism to embrace societies which had undergone revolutions of national liberation, under labels such as the "non-capitalist path."

The Destruction of Natural Resources

The third characteristic of capitalism concerns the destruction of the natural base of social production on which rests the economic calculus that characterizes the system. To cite Marx: "Capitalist production only develops the technique and the combination of the process of social production by exhausting the two sources from which all wealth springs – land and the worker."[2] This magnificent sentence written in 1863 should convince today's environmentalists that they have only rediscovered Marx, whose work they have never read.

Marx understood that the enormous growth of material production, unparalleled in history, was in part founded on the destruction of natural wealth, thus mortgaging the future of society. Thirty years ago the Japanese Marxist economist Shigeto Tsuru proposed recalculating GNP and its growth to take account of negative environmental effects. At the time, nobody listened. I myself offered a fundamental critique of an economic calculus based on a time horizon too short to merit designation as "rational." The economic rationality of capitalism ("the market") is not rational in light of the long-term interests of humanity. This is apart from the social effects of the exploitation of labour and the exclusion of entire masses of the population from participation in production.

But here again ideas have little influence on organized social consciousness. The organized workers movements in the West, the power of the Soviets in the East, and the national liberation movements of the South share the same productionist cult of growth and productivity. Even the Green movements, which have contributed to awareness of the destructive aspects of the cult of economic growth, refuse to consider the causes of environmental consequences, perhaps because questioning the rationality of markets is too frightening.

Re-introducing considerations of the limits of the planet's natural resources requires an economic calculus which is not based on the short-term profitability of capital but implies a different political and cultural civilization. We have to learn to calculate on a long-term basis, like the peasants who invested their effort in the conservation and improvement of the land, for the benefit of future generations. If the World Bank experts had been in charge, humanity would never have left the caves. Neither the improvement of land, nor the construction of transcontinental railways, nor any of the great initiatives which have transformed humanity would have been justified in terms of "cash flow" analysis taught at Harvard as the *dernier cri* in the social sciences. One cannot claim that these grand improvements were always efficient from the point of view of the preservation of the environment or the requirements of future developments. Far from it. It is inescapable that capitalism has given systematic priority to a short-term economic calculus at the cost of degradation of the natural environment.

Some Other Contradictions

The modern world is certainly not defined exclusively by the above three innovative characteristics contributed by capitalism to previous systems, and shares traits inherited from its predecessors. Some of these are no less decisive in understanding and transcending our era. I think particularly of patriarchy. It is self-evident, for example, that one can no longer reflect on issues of power without taking into account the implications of patriarchy.

But as long as social movements remain confined within narrow limits, without undertaking a radical critique of contemporary society, there can be no imagined "creative utopia," whether we call it "socialism" or some other name. Up to the present, the dominant anti-systemic, anti-capitalist forces which have imposed important transformations on the world, have been unable to imagine socialism other than "capitalism without capitalists."

END OF HISTORY? CAPITALISM MUST BE TRANSCENDED, OR ELSE ...

The indefinite expansion of capitalism is unthinkable. As Wallerstein expressed it, ferocious change together with exponential growth is like an aggressive cancer resulting in death. In time, the pursuit of this expansion will necessarily result in the progressive savaging of humanity because it is based on the economistic alienation of work and on the polarization of the world.

Economistic alienation of work strips society of minimal control of the future because responsibility for decision making is passed over to "automatic market forces," destroying the sense of society. It is not surprising that political democracy has become increasingly vacuous, ineffective, and incapable of renewal and enrichment, nor that people have responded by embracing cults of the mysterious, fundamentalist religions and sects, and various forms of instinctual affirmations of community identities. As for the second characteristic: polarization on a global scale begins to resemble a world of generalized apartheid.

More than ever, Rosa Luxemburg's "socialism or barbarism" are the alternatives. If capitalism cannot be transcended, that will be the end of history, the end of the human adventure by a sort of collective suicide or unconscious self-destruction.

Seen from a perspective that we do not yet have, and on the optimistic assumption that human reason will prevail over self-destruction, future historians will see capitalism as a parenthesis in history, a period of a two-fold accumulation of (1) material means of production and of scientific and technological knowledge enabling a mastery over nature unknown in previous ages, promising an acceptable "standard of life," but also (2) an accumulation of intellectual and moral capacities of communication, liberation of the individual, and democracy needed to transcend capitalism. Mastery over the forces of nature is of course a limited and relative concept. We cannot abolish death, anguish, uncertainty of decisions or risk. This is why the human being will remain a multi-faceted social animal, but equally also a metaphysical one. The intellectual and moral capabilities associated with material progress remain ambivalent: knowledge may serve evil as well as good, and the exercise of liberty by individuals and societies is as much a duty as a right.

Let us be optimistic and assume that reason will triumph. We now pose the political and concrete question of defining the socialist alternative and the strategies to reach this goal.

THE PEACEFUL TRANSITION TO SOCIALISM; WORLD REVOLUTION, CONSTRUCTION OF SOCIALISM IN LIBERATED COUNTRIES: THREE CONCEPTS OF SOCIALISM QUESTIONED

Marx did not concern himself with defining the future classless communist society. Rather, his analysis was aimed at unmasking the essential nature of capitalism, hidden behind the veil of money. At best, one might infer the characteristics of an alternative society by contrast. But that is all. Marx was not concerned with a strategy for the construction of socialism. As a matter of principle, he conceived communism as the product of a proletarian movement and not as a blueprint, as the utopian socialists would have it. Attention was focused exclusively on strategies of struggle against capitalism.

It was the concrete experience of the Paris Commune which provided Marx with his first answer to the question of socialism. He could not fail to reflect on this historical event. He was stimulated to arrive at some remarkable conclusions concerning, among others, the concept of a proletarian state, a democratic dictatorship, and the eventual withering away of the state. In *State and Revolution*, Lenin took up this idea on the eve of the Russian Revolution. But subsequently he concluded that it would not be possible to put these ideas into practice. Harsh realities obliged him to turn toward opposite directions.

The failure of the Paris Commune put the European working-class movement onto another path. There were two contending orientations within the Second International. Bernstein's revisionist line carried the day and evolved into social democracy. Socialist revolutionary orientation then died out, to be reborn as the Third International in historical circumstances totally different from those imagined by revolutionaries before 1914.

The propositions of Bernstein's revisionism are well known. What strikes one as important today is that the socialist society envisaged by social democracy was in fact "capitalism without capitalists." This expression was first used by Engels to describe the project of German social democracy. Whereas the imagination of the utopian socialists overflowed with questions pertaining to the civilization of our era – work, the family, relations between the sexes, power – the social democrats imagined little that was new. They shared the capitalist cult of production and productivity. They aimed to maintain most of the capitalist order, including the means to satisfy unlimited consumption by organization and discipline, hierarchy, and the division of labour. They even proposed to improve on efficiency by reducing waste due to the "anarchy of production," associated with private ownership. They were content with a socialism which would substitute state for private property. Monopolies were considered as paving the way. All that was required to achieve socialism was to bring them under public ownership. The totality of this is characterized as "capitalism without capitalists."

But the partisans of a progressive peaceful evolution to socialism were not alone in this vision of socialism. Revolutionaries shared it. Did Lenin not admire the centralized managerial bureaucracy of the German postal services? The model could thus exist in two versions: a "market socialism" where enterprises (all owned by the state) or cooperatives continued to buy and sell goods and factors of production, including labour, more or less freely; and a "state socialism" where enterprises (similarly all owned by the state) and cooperatives obeyed the dictates of a highly centralized plan. The differences are real and important, but they cannot erase the common denominator.

It is not my intention to denigrate the contribution social democracy has made to the well-being of the popular classes and to the long-term perspective of evolving beyond the strict logic of capitalism. The welfare state, introduced in one form or another in all the capitalist centres after the Second World War, is more than a historic compromise between labour and capital permitting, according to the country in question, the acquisition of social rights previously unknown in capitalist societies. It launched the legitimation of a social order no longer based on strict criteria of the profitability of capital.

The gains made by social democracy cannot be ascribed exclusively to its own organized forces nor to the objective needs of capital accumulation, as an economistic reading of the period might suggest. The historical context created by the defeat of fascism, the victory of the Soviet Union, and the appeal of communism in the years following the Second War World tilted the social balance of forces, in favour of the working class, as never before in the history of capitalism.

The vision and the strategies pursued by the revolutionary variant of socialism survived for a time within the Second International, tolerated as a minority current without influence or power. This was surprising, considering that what they offered differed little from the mainstream vision of capitalism without capitalists. Why embark on a brutal path to arrive at the same goal when everything indicated that it could be reached by peaceful evolution? Remember that the world revolution in question was expected to occur in the advanced and "civilized" centres of Europe – in Germany, France, England, Austria-Hungary, Belgium, Holland, Italy – not in the colonial peripheries.

Marginalized in the European working-class movements, the revolutionary passage to socialism manifested itself on the periphery of Europe, in Russia. Here the objectives of anti-systemic movements had been ambiguous since 1905. Was there to be a revolution for bourgeois democracy? For radical agrarian reform by peasants in rebellion? For a socialist society? This plurivalence was not a weakness but rather a strength. The vision of socialism, although limited to a minority – half intelligentsia, half worker – rose above the dominant mediocre perception of socialism as the capitalist order ameliorated by public property. Elements of the old utopian dream were mixed with Marxist orthodoxies, inspired by European working-class democratic traditions. At the start the revolutionary project was not one of state socialism or capitalism without capitalists. When it unexpectedly became a historic reality in October 1917, it was not "the spark to set aflame the plains" nor the "first explosion in the weakest chain" destined to be followed by revolutions in the most advanced countries. It was an expression of another anti-systemic force, representing the refusal of the people of the periphery to submit to the exigencies of capitalist polarization.

Reality dictated the passage from world revolution to the construction of socialism in one country. Stalin cannot be reproached for that choice, because there was no alternative. The theory said: revolution or nothing. Could the Russians have committed suicide for the sake of faith in a world revolution which was not on the agenda? What could be held against Stalin was the decision to maintain or return to the narrow horizon of social democratic realism which could not imagine a socialism other than capitalism without capitalists. The utopians of 1917 were dismissed in favour of realists whom, under different circumstances, the Second International could have recognized as their own. That choice determined all the rest. The entire socialist project lost its meaning when it was subordinated to the priority of "catching up" by accelerating the rate of accumulation. The exploitation of the peasantry in state-controlled cooperatives served to finance so-called socialist primitive accumulation. The rupture of the alliance of workers and peasants which had produced the triumph of the revolution opened the way to a despotic dictatorship in the name of the proletariat. The bureaucracy was freed from all control to implement the authoritarian planning of state socialism.

The debate then revolves around the reasons for the choice. Could it have been different? Could the revolution have moved faster toward a democratic communism and the disappearance of the state? Or more slowly by prolonging the compromise with capital of the NEP? Or differently, faster in certain directions, more slowly in others?

In China the objective of the construction of socialism was never in doubt from the start of the communist revolution. It was never expected that revolutions in Japan or the United States could assist the Chinese people to overcome their economic backwardness. There was never a period of hesitation, as in the first years following the Russian Revolution. On the contrary, Mao proclaimed from the start that it was both necessary and possible to construct socialism in a backward country by means of permanent revolution by stages. Radical agrarian and other bourgeois reforms were carried out under "the direction of the proletariat." As in Russia, private enterprise was nationalized and rural cooperatives set up. Even though these changes were, I believe, introduced more successfully in China, they were not fundamentally different from capitalism without capitalists.

The Chinese communists declined to borrow the Soviet model because they concluded that the USSR was constructing capitalism rather than socialism. Maoists tried to do things differently, to follow a different path, one with a slower rate of accumulation which would reduce strain on the worker-peasant alliance and foster progress in the area of communist ideology by means of the cultural revolution and a reorganization of political power – a promise never fulfilled. Ultimately, neither approach worked; the Maoist project was abandoned in 1980 and the Soviet model disintegrated by the 1990s.

The principal lesson here is that history has showed that the construction of socialism in question was not irreversible. The *étatisme*, which I once called the "Soviet mode of production," did not constitute a stable model but a chaotic and conflicting transition which might have developed slowly and progressively toward socialism, to revert to capitalism pure and simple in the former Soviet Union and Eastern Europe.

These setbacks were not the only ones. Other concepts of socialism have not been treated by history. All the more or less faithful copies of the Soviet model (with the sole exception of Vietnam and Cuba) and other more distantly related African or Asian socialisms had ceased to exist, even before their abandonment by Moscow. Even western welfare socialism, which seemed permanently anchored in consciousness and social reality, has been destabilized by the collapse of the Soviet model. For the time being, the neoliberal offensive has successfully set back the clock in the western world.

These serious and general failures have cast doubt on the very idea of socialism. Is it an unrealizable utopia, in the common meaning of the word? Is humanity condemned to self-destruction by a capitalist "end of history"? The simultaneous crumbling of Sovietism and abandonment of Maoism has eliminated the idea of competition – whether by violent conflict or by peaceful co-existence – between two economic, political and social systems embodied in two blocs of states, Zhdanov's "two camps" of 1948. That page has been turned. The question now is: What is the nature of the struggle between socialism and capitalism in our world today?

RETURNING TO THE QUESTION OF SOCIALISM

Socialism has no meaning if it does not offer a civilization different from that produced by capitalism, if it cannot transcend the principal contradictions of our contemporary world outlined above. Socialism must be based on a civilization free from economistic alienation, free from patriarchy, which has solved its relationship with nature, which develops democracy beyond the limitations imposed by the separation of the economic from the political, and where globalization ceases to produce, indeed reverses, polarization.

If this is the objective, the struggle for socialism in our era must meet four major challenges confronting the people of the world.

The challenge of the market It is a question neither of substituting bureaucratic centralized planning – which has nothing to do with socialism – for all forms of market economy nor of subordinating society to the constraints of the market, as the dominant ideologies propose and as implemented by policies they inform. Rather it is a question of clarifying the objectives and the means (judicial, administrative, organizational, social, and political) to confine the market to serve society and assure social progress (full employment, the largest possible measure of equity, etc.). Various mixed forms of property (private, public, state-owned, cooperatives, and others) will certainly continue for a long time.

The challenge of the "world economy" The false debate whether one should accept integration into the world economy and attempt only to improve one's position within the hierarchy, or whether it is to be rejected altogether, must give way to a discussion of the real unavoidable constraints globalization has imposed on policies of autonomous social, national, and political development. In other words it is a matter of utilizing the margins of possibility to invert external/internal relations by refusing unilateral adjustments to exterior constraints, adjusting the international system to the real requirements of our own development. This is what I mean by *delinking*, which is one of the principal arenas of action to achieve necessary radical reform.

The challenge of democracy It is neither a matter of regarding so-called liberal bourgeois democracy as the "end of history" nor of embracing populist practices. Rather it is a matter of re-enforcing political democracy (fundamental human rights, individual liberties, pluralism, the rule of law) with the concrete articulation of social rights (including the rights to work and to control the economic decision making) which define the rules within which markets should operate.

The challenge of national and cultural pluralism It is neither a question of creating homogenous communities (nation, ethnic group or religious community) with exclusive exercise of power nor of denying that pluralism in this domain requires respect of difference and diversity. Strategies of liberation should aim to provide the largest possible political space for the co-existence and interaction of the most diverse assortment of communities. The margins of autonomy which popular forces can and should mobilize to effect radical reforms depend on concrete local and international conditions. It is the role of popular struggles to progressively enlarge and extend the scope of autonomy. Effective strategies of action must seriously address the challenges described above. The objective is to bring into existence a civilization which advances qualitatively beyond the boundaries of capitalism. I will not return to the basic ideological dimensions of this project. Our (Marxist, I believe) critique of capitalism and of historical attempts to transcend it have been sufficiently well explained. I insist only on the unity of an analysis which can bring together, in a coherent whole, the requirements of democracy, the need to end the divorce of economics from politics, and the mastery of decisions integrating long-term considerations and globalization.

At stake is an ideology and a culture with a universal vocation. The reader will recognize my well-known hostility to culturalism understood as the rejection of a universalist perspective in favour of supposedly different paths leading to the development of different communities. I reject all such currently fashionable appeal founded on ethnicism and religious diversity as profoundly reactionary. They represent a step back from what capitalism has achieved in the direction of the universal. For the globalization it has imposed is not only technological, commercial, and geopolitical: it is also cultural. This is why I conceived the dominant world culture as capitalist, not as western.

If capitalist globalization presents strong negative traits of polarization, it also offers positive dimensions such as the liberation of individuals and societies which, even if embryonic, incomplete, and deformed by the dominant logic of capital, are no less real. The negative effects of polarization do not manifest exclusively in the economy – the contrasts of rich and poor peoples – but are complemented by the contrast between political democracy and its absence, a contrast that has associated the arrogance of the West with the neurotic confusion of capitalist culture and its apparent expressions ("European and Christian").

These negative aspects of capitalist globalization cannot be overcome by a return to the ancient world of diverse ideological expressions of tributary societies, to use my terminology. They can only be overcome by moving forward to the construction of a universalist socialist culture.

It should not be necessary to explain that the universality of the project does not entail leveling everything to the lowest common denominator, as is the case with capitalist universalism – Coca Cola for all; ethnic and religious hatreds to go with it. Socialist universalism, by contrast, is necessarily built by and from the contribution of all people, whose diversity is an enriching element of this common understanding.

In the light of this vision of a universal culture, historic attempts to surpass capitalism were neither insignificant nor ridiculous. Far from it. Western social democratic society is certainly not the most odious we have known. On the contrary, it is the most advanced, sympathetic, and humane, even if this is a judgment viewed from the "inside," forgetting that viewed from the periphery it has often been associated with imperialist attitudes, pure and simple. And if societies of "really existing socialism" had some repugnant aspects, seen from the "outside" they have been the most generous in their support of anti-fascist struggles and national liberation movements of the peoples of the periphery. Their achievements have not been negligible or limited to material progress. Tito's Yugoslavia overcame the hostility of ethnic components. The Chinese live infinitely better than the Indians. The wild capitalism in Russia today is not only harsher in terms of the material conditions of the majority of the people, but does not even guarantee democracy. The neo-comprador regimes in the Third World are worse, in many respects, than the populist regimes which preceded them. The examples multiply – without end.

All this goes to show that "capitalism without capitalists," whether the social democratic market or the state version, was neither absurd or without value. It represented bourgeois ideology at its most progressive stage. Our age dislikes the French Revolution, and Jacobism – its most advanced expression – even more. Today, reactionary cults of communitarian specificities and hatred of universalism are *à la mode*. Nevertheless, Jacobism represented a step beyond the simple requirements of the establishment of bourgeois power. It expressed the utopian aspirations of the common people and reflected the avant-garde of the Enlightenment. Jacobism invented the idea of the republic of citizens and even discovered that economic liberalism (the "market") was the enemy of democracy.

Capitalism without capitalists is a late expression of this logic of surpassing capitalism, however fragile and incomplete. It implies the powerful intervention of the state as organizer of rationality with a universal reach, an unfashionable intervention in our age of all reactionary anti-statism. One is quick to confound with facile condemnation the mercantilist étatism of Colbert, Bismark's Prussian Hegelian state, Soviet Russia which inherited Czarist autocracy, or Mao as inheritor of the Middle Kingdom. But what has replaced the citizen state? Ethnic nations, religious communities in combination with the market, without the state? The jungle, pure and simple, complete with the mutual hatred of the communities in question? These are also utopias, but reactionary ones precisely because they are anti-universalist, whereas capitalism accepts and even imposes globalization.

If the alternative to crude capitalism is the construction of a civilized socialist world, the path will necessarily be long because what is at issue is the building of a new civilization. A possible reproach of previous attempts to construct socialism is that they reduced the task to the implementation of a few reforms – principally the abolition of private property. Important as these reforms were, they were not enough. In the 1920s, the Russian Revolution was searching its own way forward, but the termination of the NEP and collectivization in 1930 set it on the path of capitalism without capitalists. Six years later, Stalin proclaimed that the construction of socialism was complete. In China the popular armies entered Beijing in 1949. The land reform of 1952 was soon followed by collectivization. It was announced in 1957 that the construction of socialism had been achieved. Surely a new civilization cannot be constructed in five or six years!

The long transition on which we now embark calls for a discussion of strategies by stages. In the light of new perspectives, experiences of the past, including social democracy and market socialism, could constitute elements of such a strategy of stages.

A NEW CONCEPT OF THE TRANSITION

The above considerations have led me to conclude that the theory which maintains that socialism cannot develop within capitalism in the manner in which capitalism developed within feudalism before breaking out of its shell, will have to be relativized.

Just as three centuries of mercantilism (1500–1800) represented a long transition from feudalism to capitalism, during which the two systems co-existed, we can contemplate a long transition from world capitalism to world socialism, during which the logic of capital accumulation coexists in conflict with the logic of social needs.

Marx believed that capitalism would rapidly accomplish its historic mission of integrating all the planet's societies within the framework of one relatively homogenized economic and social system, thus reducing all contradictions to the single one between the bourgeoisie and proletariat. This was to prepare the transition of humanity toward the new classless society. Marx believed that capitalism and socialism were incapable of coexisting even conflictually within the same society, separated, as it were, by a kind of Great Wall of China. Nevertheless, this vision did not exclude the possibility of conflictual coexistence for a period of time between these two parts of society, the one still capitalist, the other already socialist, on the condition that this period be short. In Marx's view, completed socialism could only be planetary.

My analysis of really existing capitalism knocks down this Great Wall. Reality is more complex. Indeed, the accent is on the conflict between capitalist and socialist logic as they exist within the framework of really existing capitalism – in contrast to the ideal capitalist mode of production on a world scale. Capitalism as it concretely exists functions only on the condition that anti-systemic forces permit it to overcome its inherent contradictions. Second, world capitalist expansion is polarizing because it continuously produces these very anti-systemic and anti-polarizing forces.

Early in my work, I came to the conclusion that expanded capitalist reproduction was only possible if real salaries increased with productivity. As its unilateral logic does not permit this, capitalism is threatened by permanent stagnation, which would make it an impossible system. This absurd contradiction is only overcome through historic events outside its logic (thus the meshing of the great phases of capitalist expansion with revolutionary and imperial wars, colonizations, the German and Italian unifications, successive technological revolutions) or else paradoxically through the anti-systemic logic of class struggle, by means of which the working class along with peasants and other producers succeed in imposing increases in remuneration for work. This dialectic associating the logic of accumulation with that of social distribution of revenue culminated, in the age of monopolies and national productive systems (1920–70), in the historic compromise of the welfare state, a social arrangement presently in crisis due to globalization, which has eroded the power of national productive systems and has caused the general weakening of the working classes in the overall political balance. Thus capitalist accumulation is also in crisis.

In its struggle against the anti-systemic logic developed by the exploited classes, threatened national capitalism escapes in external expansion, producing polarizing globalization. Dominant capital compensates for what it lost in the most advanced centres through what it gains by submitting – however not destroying – the original precapitalist forms which it finds in its path, thus peripherizing backward zones. World capitalism did not inherit an original heterogeneity. Rather, it ceaselessly recreates it to its benefit. Marx's law of accumulation formulated in terms of pauperization, attenuated and suppressed in the advanced centres, finds itself operative on the global scale. However on this level of really existing capitalism, the law of accumulation does not operate within the framework of the pure mode of capitalist production. Rather it takes place within the overall network of centres and peripheries which constitute really existing capitalism. This polarization/pauperization is obviously not acceptable to the peoples who are its victims. Like the working class in the centre, people in the periphery express their anti-systemic tendencies – with the difference that their struggles usually take the form of national liberation movements and/or socialist revolution.

From this perspective, I propose a rereading of the history of capitalism as a succession of phases. Sometimes the unilateral logic dominates and the system undergoes a worldwide expansion, other times the anti-systemic revolt of the peripheries imposes itself. The nineteenth century was a long phase of the first kind; the period from 1917 to 1990, is the second.

The legitimate question which must be raised at this stage of our development is: If capitalism has this extraordinary capacity to adjust to these anti-systemic forces which are the products of its own development, why can't capitalism survive eternally? If we extend those successive phases of growth and decline, submission and regression of capitalism in the periphery, can we imagine a homogenized world built on a less developed capitalism? Marx would have been right in the long run: the law of accumulation homogenizes the world.

So far, the system has not responded this way. Due to the resistance of anti-systemic forces, polarization has not gradually diminished. Rather it has become worse. Similarly, although earnings have increased with productivity in the centres over the long term, alienation in the workplace has increased: witness the "crisis of work" in contemporary society. In other words, the system can only persist by attenuating its three principal contradictions. As it reinforces them, the system is fatally condemned to becoming progressively more unbearable and explosive.

However intolerable, this does mean that capitalism will be succeeded by the rational response – socialism – as by a force of nature. Here I return to what I proposed twenty years ago regarding the dynamic of social transformation. At the time, I suggested the choice was between revolution or decadence. By revolution, I suggested a historic process of transformation (not excluding radical evolution) whereby social forces, guided by a clear understanding of the objectives, drive the struggle against the old order. I gave as examples the passage of the systems of the *ancien régime* in Europe to capitalist modernity. On the other hand, in the absence of ideological consciousness and political will which defines the project of the new society, the transformation proceeds hesitantly in a fog. This then opens the way for decadence, as exemplified by the passage from antiquity to feudalism in the Europe built on the ruins of the decadent Roman Empire.

One is left with the question: Will capitalism be surpassed by a new social project or simply by the haphazard result of partial struggles, of a thousand and one motives more often than not in conflict with each other? The emergence of decadence is always a possibility. However, given our concern and the great capacity for destruction available to modern systems, there runs a high risk of self-destruction, what I refer to as collective suicide. Thus the only choice is Gramsci's optimism of the will. This means equipping social movements of opposition with clear awareness and appropriate strategies to struggle against the unacceptable conditions of really existing capitalism. I do not intend here to propose an "active" global "plan." I will be satisfied with opening a debate on some early reflections on the subject.

The present generalized disarray cannot last. The facts demonstrate the absurdity of managing global society as if it were a supermarket. In record time this project has produced a maximum number of catastrophes and has driven societies into an impasse of stagnation and unbearable regression. The arrogance of neoliberal discourse is floundering. Already in a number of Eastern European countries, the former Communist parties – for what they are worth – have been voted back into power. In France, the extensive popular protest of December 1995, the first in the West which dared to reject neoliberalism outright, signals a possible reversal within Europe. In certain countries of the Third World such as Brazil, Mexico, Korea, Philippines, and South Africa, popular democratic anti-systematic movements have made their mark and may also represent the beginning of a new discourse. On the other hand, the sirens of illusory and criminal responses have succeeded in attracting large segments of popular movements. Thus the reality of our time is also distinguished by neoconservative and fascist tendencies, excesses of ethnic delirium, chauvinism and nationalist narrow-mindedness, as well as religious fundamentalism as responses to the illegitimacy of the powers that be. We are heading toward violent confrontations between the left and the right. The new left could win the battle in many countries in both the North and the South, on the condition that it remobilizes around appropriate strategies embedded in a clear vision of an alternative socialist society. I would like to reflect on what conditions would be required for this to be achieved in a variety of situations.

For the peripheries in general, for a number of years I have been proposing a step toward the development of a national popular and democratic alliance. Without returning to the details of the proposition, I wish to recall its four basic features. First, the redefinition of economic and social anti-*comprador* policies, national in the sense that they reflect the reality of conflict between their objectives and the dominant logic of the expansion of the global economy. Second, the identification of the social forces which have a common interest in putting these policies into action as well as conflicts of interest which generate opposition among these social forces ("contradictions among the people"). Third, the construction of democratic forms of organization which would permit the resolution of such conflicts and lead to a common struggle against the enemy, both internal and external. Fourth, the reinforcement of interior fronts by resisting both regional and global strategies, thereby forcing the global system to readjust, contrary to what the system proposes, which is none other than the unilateral adjustment to the demands of the global economy.

In my view, there already exists concrete forces moving in this direction, forces that are more than embryonic or mere intellectual debates. The Workers Party in Brazil, the democratic, neo-Zapatista opposition to the PRI in Mexico, the democratic forces of mass action in Korea, the Philippines, and elsewhere, the ANC-PC-OSATU bloc in South Africa (notwithstanding the dominant liberal ideology of the government and the Nationalist Party) have all created space for coherent and consistent action by the left.

I also suggested that this perspective would apply to the new political environment in China. In the Chinese context, I emphasize the strengths of "national and popular" post-Maoist strategy (three positive trends: mastery of external relations, social redistribution of revenue, and the reinforcement of interprovincial complementaries; but there are also weaknesses – the critical "negative" being the absence of a concept of democracy and the persistent adherence to the party state as defined by the Third International). The future will tell how these contradictions resolve themselves. Either they will reinforce the national bourgeois content of the project with a view to catching up and transforming China; the strategies of adversaries, Japan and the U.S.A., will win, resulting in the division of China; or the national and popular aspirations of post-Maoist China will stabilize themselves in what is officially referred to as "market socialism." While this last scenario is not ideal in the creation of socialism as I have defined it, it nevertheless constitutes a positive strategic step in the long transition toward socialism.

Despite the marked specificities of the capitalist centres of Japan, Europe, and North America, the historic parties of the left have suffered a common fate (the Social Democratic and Communist parties). They all have in common the explosion of new forms of social movements, of which feminism and environmentalism are probably the most important, without neglecting ethnic and religious revivals. Some of these movements have become parliamentary political parties such as the Greens in certain European countries, without really becoming new oppositional political forces that challenge capitalism. Other movements support right-wing offensives. Some movements are clearly progressive, as on principle they attack one of the most reactionary characteristics of our society. The feminist movement must be especially singled out for its militancy and resistance. In passing, I note that 1968 represents an important date in the history of advanced capitalist societies, giving the protest against the alienation of work a depth it has never since lost.

The fundamental question is whether the combined forces which represent the left in Western civil society – parties, unions, movements – will be able to produce the new social project necessary for the development of appropriate strategies. For Europe, the success or failure of leftist strategies is embedded in the European project. Will the European left, for the most part remain prisoner of the vision of the right, of the European Common Market, or will it succeed in producing an integrated, progressive political and social project? The situation is obviously different in the United States, where the bi-polarization imposed by the Republican-Democrat electoral split shows no sign of disappearing. In Japan, the conservative single-party system remains; signs of decadence do not appear to open the way to alternatives.

In all cases, even under the most favourable conditions for the mobilization of the left, the question remains: will anti-systemic forces simply impose mere adjustments on capitalism that will allow the system to continue despite its internal contradictions, or can there be genuine transformation? At that point, we may say that an important step will be taken toward the long transition to socialism.

NOTES

1 Translation from French by Tom Levitt, Kari Polanyi Levitt, and Marguerite Mendell.

2 *Capital*. Trans. Joseph Roy, rev. Karl Marx. 10th ed. (Paris: Sociales Paris):182.

11 Confluences

KARI POLANYI LEVITT

Much time has passed since we gathered in Montreal in October 1998 to celebrate the seventy-fifth anniversary of Gregory Baum and Kari Levitt, an event attended by friends and well wishers, old and new, including Canadian and Caribbean colleagues who found time to travel to Montreal and prepare important presentations. The day was full and long, and did not permit reflection on the papers by colleagues whose work and friendship is intimately woven into the fabric of my perambulating life. Released from constraints of brevity, I welcome this opportunity to record the web of confluences which has linked my work in Canada with work in the Caribbean, and more recently with the intellectual legacy of my father, Karl Polanyi. My warmest thanks and deepest appreciation go to Margie Mendell, whose collaboration in the foundation and work of the Karl Polanyi Institute is internationally respected and valued. Margie also made it possible for me to teach in Jamaica for most of the 1990s without losing contact with the work of the Institute. Finally, she had the original idea for the symposium that celebrated Gregory and me.

The Caribbean is small, perhaps insignificant in the larger context of the "South." For most Canadians, it is beach, a winter tourist destination. But my Caribbean is the place where Africa, Asia, and Europe have created a unique culture in the Americas, with commonalities transcending differences of language, political institutions, and official ideologies. The island archipelago and the coastal littoral of the Caribbean Sea, and its diasporas in Europe and North America, are "a Planet collapsed";[1] "a Canvass of the World."[2] Peoples transplanted here reassembled in complex multi-layered – yet unmistakably Caribbean – societies of diverse ancestry, religion, and language. Relatively poor in terms of material wealth, the Caribbean is rich in the texture of everyday life and explosive in all areas of creative expression. It is a world – and it is a village. Wherever you travel in the Caribbean, you find the same familiar tastes, smells, sounds, vibrations. The late George Beckford described the whole Caribbean as One Nation. The vision of the Caribbean as a *sui generis* civilization with its own muse, its own ways of seeing and being, shaped by the legacy of the sugar plantation, this "Enterprise of the Indies," as Lloyd Best has called it, has nourished my spirit for the past forty years.

In the first part of this paper, I take advantage of this opportunity to recall events and confluences of life and work in Montreal and the West Indies and to reflect on my state of cultural and geographical "betweenity" – a condition familiar to all immigrants. In my case, the spaces span Central Europe whence I came, England where I grew up and went to university, Montreal which has been my home and academic base since 1961, and the Caribbean, which has informed my engagement with problems of development since I first set foot in the West Indies in 1960. In the second part of the paper I address issues raised at the symposium by colleagues from the Caribbean and Canada, and reflect briefly on the important contribution to the symposium by Samir Amin. It is my hope that what emerges will tie the strands of ideas into the semblance of a coherent perspective on my professional concerns of the past forty years: how peoples and societies can secure economic livelihood, eliminate poverty, indignity, and injustice, and protect the heritage of cultural and environmental diversity from plunder and destruction by the global reach of unconstrained capitalism. This is my definition of "development." It is unnecessary to enhance it by adjectives like "human," "participatory" or "sustainable" because without these attributes there is no meaningful development. As for "reclaiming democracy," the theme of this book, we must bear in mind that most regions of the ex-colonial world have never experienced democracy as we know it in Europe or Canada. This is so even where the trappings of Westminster-style political institutions are in place, as in Jamaica, but the legacy of slavery has not been extinguished.

THE MAGIC OF MONTREAL

The timing of the establishment of the Karl Polanyi Institute of Political Economy at Concordia University in 1987 was utterly timely. Although nobody anticipated the historic events which crashed the Berlin Wall and the Soviet empire in 1989, the rise of a hegemonic neoliberal ideology in the 1980s prepared the ground for a rediscovery of Karl Polanyi's historical and anthropological critique of market economy. His work is gaining ever-growing recognition, reflected in the response to our efforts to build an international network of scholars and social activists seeking alternatives to the false utopia of "universal capitalism." For me personally, the Institute has squared the circle, in a closure which enabled me to revisit my Central European roots without loosening the ties that bind to the Caribbean.

I was delighted that Mel Watkins, Duncan Cameron, and all other Canadian friends old and new came to share the celebration with Lloyd Best, Norman Girvan, and Michael Witter. None are strangers to Montreal. Nor is Samir Amin, who was unable to attend, but sent a paper which revisits issues of capitalism and socialism in the search for civilizational transformation. We first met in 1972 in Dakar, when Norman Girvan was located at IDEP, but our friendship really dates to a conference in Jamaica in 1989, where we discovered essential similarities of his world of thought and that of my father. Samir Amin is a firm friend of the Karl Polanyi Institute and attended our conferences in Milan (1990) and Vienna (1994). In Jamaica, we visited George Beckford at his country house in White Horses a year before his death. Beckford also was a frequent visitor to Montreal, where he studied agricultural economics at the MacDonald campus of McGill before obtaining his Ph.D. at Stanford and joining the economics department of the Jamaica campus of the University of the West Indies. He was a pillar of the New World Movement, founded by Lloyd Best in Guyana in 1962. I know that Beckford was with us in spirit in October 1998.

There is a magic in Montreal which, in good times and bad, has sustained my existential state of "betweenity," noted in a characteristically insightful observation by Lloyd Best. The city is unique in its cosmopolitan embrace of diversity and difference, with a transplanted European flavour. We are all minorities here. The French are a fragile minority in a vast English-speaking continent; the English are a minority in French Quebec; and all the ethnic communities of Quebec are twice minorities. I am comfortable here with my "betweenity." McGill University has historically been enriched by a large number of foreign – including West Indian – students. It provided the academic base from which I was able to extend my work to the Caribbean in a strange confluence of circumstances. It was my good fortune to have combined engagement in public affairs in Canada with teaching and research in Trinidad, Jamaica, Guyana, Suriname, Grenada, and Haiti, and with visits to Cuba, Barbados, St Lucia, St Vincent, and the Dominican Republic. Countless departures and arrivals have long blunted the edge of culture shock in both directions. I am now equally at home in Kingston and Port of Spain as in Montreal. But I could never live in any other Canadian city.

Although they did not know each other at the time, Lloyd Best and Mel Watkins played key roles in the publication of *Silent Surrender* in 1970. At Lloyd's insistence an early version of this essay was published in the *New World Quarterly* in 1968. When a Canadian publisher showed interest, Mel rescued the manuscript from a trashing by an unsympathetic reader, and wrote the introduction.[3] Watkins was the principal author of the Watkins Report on Foreign Ownership, commissioned by Walter Gordon. This report and *Silent Surrender* were influential in the formation of a generation of young Canadians. Regrettably, the efforts of Walter Gordon, Mel Watkins, Stephen Hymer, Abe Rotstein, and many others, including myself, failed to turn the tide of Canadian nationalism toward a social project of self-reliant development. Incidentally, Rotstein and Hymer, a brilliant economist who died prematurely in a car accident, were both born and raised in Montreal. So also was Joe Levitt, my former husband and father of my children.

Montreal was at its most glorious in the year of Expo 67. The Trinidad pavilion, with a steel orchestra on an artificial island, vied with the Czech pavilion as a major attraction of this truly magnificent celebration of Canada (and Montreal) at its very best. For Canada, it has been downhill ever since. The 1960s marked a high tide of social and political activism culminating in 1968, when a wave of anti-establishment protest swept through the Western world. In the streets of Paris and Prague, at the Olympics in Mexico City, in civil rights actions in the United States, and demonstrations for Quebec sovereignty in Montreal, the post-war generation of youth rose to assert demands for justice, freedom, peace (in Vietnam), and inclusion in the making of their futures. In 1968, Pierre Trudeau was swept to power in a general election, and the stage was set for the confrontation of October 1970, when Canada invoked the War Measures Act. The Canadian army occupied Montreal, and hundreds of Quebec artists and intellectuals were arrested as suspects in an "apprehended insurrection."

Montreal was also the scene of the historic Black Writers Conference of 1968, when Caribbean intellectuals, including some residing in London and the United States, gathered in an atmosphere dominated by the rise of radical black power politics. On his return from Montreal, the brilliant Guyanese scholar Walter Rodney was denied re-entry to Jamaica, where he was a university teacher, known and respected by students and urban ghetto youth. Riots brought the country to the brink of revolution, which was averted only by the election with a large majority of Michael Manley in 1972.

Another spinoff from that conference was local. A charge of discrimination in examination grades by Caribbean students at Sir George Williams College (now Concordia University) escalated into the occupation of the computer area, the burning of computer cards, eviction of students by the riot police, and criminal charges. Several McGill students, including Rosie Douglas, who became Prime Minister of Dominica before his recent untimely death, were involved.

I was approached to take a group of parents and faculty to meet with Minister Mitchell Sharpe. I clearly recall that I told the Minister that if justice were not done and seen to be done in the case of the Caribbean students, there could be consequences detrimental to Canadian investments in the region. A scribe sitting in a corner of the huge office recorded the proceedings.

When I arrived in Trinidad with my family in the autumn of 1969 to take up an IMF-financed appointment as statistical advisor on national accounts to the Government of Trinidad, I learned that visiting Canadian dignitaries and Canadian banks had been the object of student protests. By February 1970, street demonstrations were a daily occurrence in Port of Spain, as the youth of the city turned out in their thousands to proclaim "power to the people" in carnival-like peaceful marches. I witnessed the return of the Trinidad contingent of Sir George Williams students, assisted by their government to come home, and warmly welcomed by the demonstrators. Although I was a mere observer of these events, I have no doubt that the Canadian security authorities were adding more entries to my file.

But I have run ahead of the story. My engagement with the Caribbean goes back to December 1960. The person directly responsible was Professor B.S. Keirstead.

FIRST ENCOUNTER WITH THE WEST INDIES

I met Professor Keirstead as a graduate student at the University of Toronto, where he was in exile from McGill following a blazing row with the administration of the university. At McGill, Keirstead had built an exemplary economics department, staffed by creative scholars, with a social conscience and predominantly left-leaning political views. He was an excellent teacher and directed me toward the problems of underdeveloped regions, specifically the Maritime provinces of Canada, whence he originally came, and whose problems continued to engage his interest. I spent two summers in Fredericton, New Brunswick, working for the Atlantic Provinces Economic Council. During that time I complemented extensive reading of the works of Harold Innis and other material on Canadian economic history with the early "development economics" literature – Arthur Lewis, Ben Higgins, and the classic pioneering collection by Agarwala and Singh, first published in India in the mid 1950s. I found this literature very exciting, and regretted that I was stuck in Toronto. I wished to find a way to use my economics education to participate in the "development" of recently de-colonized regions.

The opportunity came when Professor Keirstead spent a sabbatical at the then University College of the West Indies in Jamaica. At the invitation of Arthur Lewis, he undertook a study of the inter-island shipping service on behalf of the Federal Government of the West Indies. A graduate student was sent for. The next three weeks transformed my life. I arrived at the Mona Campus and was soon dispatched to Trinidad to examine the cargo manifests in the dusty archives of the Furness and Withy shipping company. It was Christmas 1960. I was enchanted by the old-time festivities of bottle and spoon music, parang, pan around-the-neck steelbands, and the fêtes. At night under mosquito net, I read West Indian novels – Selvon, Lamming, Naipaul, etc. I discovered much that was familiar from my growing up years in England: Cambridge and LSE graduates, cricket, and expressions I had not heard in thirteen years of life in North America. I felt like a bird released from a cage. I fell in love with the Caribbean, a love affair beyond the reach of any man to disappoint.

It was a time of high hopes for the transition from political colonialism to independence. The Cuban Revolution was recent and proximate. In Trinidad, I met chief economist William Demas, who became a lifelong friend and telephone companion. We shared an interest in the economics of development and a growing dissatisfaction with trends toward irrelevant abstraction in academic economics. I met Lloyd Best on the Mona Campus, where he was the youngest West Indian appointed to a university post. His irreverence was already legendary. Professor Keirstead extended moral support to him and other young West Indians seeking their rightful place in a university dominated by expatriate staff. He introduced Lloyd Best to Francois Perroux in Paris, who was indirectly instrumental in his appointment to a United Nations mission to assist Cheddi Jagan with a development plan in Guyana. I met Alister McIntyre, lecturing in international trade on the Mona campus, subsequently Director of the Institute of Social and Economic Research. In 1964 I met George Beckford. A stream of UWI graduates came to McGill, including among many others, Hugh O'Neale, Adlith Brown, Edwin Carrington, and Ainsworth Harewood.

Radical anti-colonialism and pan-Caribbean nationalism contributed to the appeal of the New World Groups Lloyd Best initiated in Guyana in 1962, even though the movement was confined to the English speaking Caribbean and "regionalism" was effectively limited to the component territories of the West Indies. It is interesting to recall, however, that when the old order crumbled in Cuba, and Trinidad demanded the return of the (American) base in Chaguaramas in 1960, Lloyd Best castigated Dr Eric Williams for "missing the chance of a lifetime" of declaring Chaguaramas to be national property, proclaiming independence, and joining Cuba in nationalizing the sugar industry. Imagine the impact of two small nations at opposite ends of the Caribbean confronting "the biggest bully" ever known to nations. The Caribbean would have emerged from the struggle as morally and politically integrated as it has always been culturally – thanks to sugar, mercantilism, and imperial domination. But the time will come again. Change is a slow process and the consciousness built by work and life today will tell in the politics of tomorrow.

That was forty years ago. Interestingly, now that Cuba is passing through a difficult transition, and the small countries of the Caribbean are threatened by marginalization in a world of economic megablocs, the Caribbean region is drawing closer together. Haiti and Suriname have joined CARICOM, the Dominican Republic and Haiti have been accepted into Cariforum, and the twenty-five member countries of the Association of Caribbean States (ACS) have agreed to establish the Greater Caribbean region as a "Zone of Cooperation," starting with the "Sustainable Tourism Zone of the Caribbean." Congratulations to Norman Girvan, now serving as Secretary General of ACS, for bringing the vision of One Caribbean Nation a few steps closer.

The New World Movement marked a high point of post-colonial intellectual ferment on the campuses of the University of the West Indies. Independence was the key. It was a movement to free the mind from mimicry of metropolitan styles in everything from dress, food, and hairstyles to political philosophy and economic models of development. The New World groups were informal forums, open to all. The project was to theorize Caribbean reality in terms of Caribbean experience and historical process and to build political commitment. The objective was to provide intellectual leadership to transform Caribbean economies to become self-reliant, defining their own needs and how to meet them with their own resources.

New World Groups operated in Jamaica, Trinidad, Guyana, Puerto Rico, Antigua, New York – and Montreal. My home in Outremont was the meeting place of the Montreal group. The Montreal New World Group participated in the organization of a West Indian Conference in 1966, with George Lamming as keynote speaker. It was here that Lloyd Best presented his seminal paper on "Independent Thought and Caribbean Freedom." Following the conference, we were shattered by the death of two of its principal organizers in a tragic car accident. Hugh O'Neale was twenty-eight, Alvin Johnson thirty-three years old when they left us. The Barbados Independence issue of *New World* was dedicated to their memory. It was my first encounter with death.

The New World Movement did not survive pressures to engage in direct political action in the turbulent 1970s. Marxism and Black Power were more attractive to revolutionary youth than the more moderate national development agendas of *New World*. Lloyd dissolved the Trinidad group in 1969 and founded his own Tapia Movement, and the *Trinidad and Tobago Review*, an excellent cultural journal published by his Trinidad and Tobago Institute.

APPOINTMENT TO McGILL UNIVERSITY

My encounter with the West Indies is not the only debt I owe to Burton Keirstead. He was also instrumental in my appointment to a teaching position at McGill University in 1961, on the invitation of Jack Weldon, the intellectual pillar of the department until his untimely death in 1988. The chair of the then joint Department of Economics and Political Science was Professor James Mallory. He was a man of sterling integrity and courage, displayed on many occasions, including my appointment, at a time when McCarthyism was far from dead. He knew that I came with considerable political baggage. I had spent my first ten years in Canada in Toronto, where my children were born in 1952 and 1954 and I was engaged in trade union and left-wing political activities. In 1957 I resigned from the Communist Party, following the crushing of the Hungarian revolution of 1956 by Soviet tanks, and enrolled in post-graduate studies at the University of Toronto.

This was also the year my father's cancer was diagnosed, and his multidisciplinary research program at Columbia was not renewed. The long arm of McCarthyism directly affected our family. My mother was banned from entering the United States for her anti-war activism in Hungary in the First World War, and her anti-fascist activities in Communist parties in Austria in the 1930s. For this reason my parents made their home in Canada, near Toronto, whence my father commuted to Colombia University in New York. After his retirement, his graduate students commuted from the United States to Ontario to continue research work on economic anthropology. The culture of fear was so pervasive that my father was not once invited to give a seminar at the University of Toronto's Department of Political Economy. We were informed by Marshall MacLuhan, a frequent visitor to my parents' home, that the chair of the department feared losing his U.S.-based foundation grant.

As a junior member of the economics department I lectured almost all undergraduate courses at least once. My real interest however was techniques of economic planning. My Ph.D. thesis, never completed, evolved into an ambitious statistical exercise of the construction – and updating – of input-output tables for each of the four Atlantic provinces. The project was intended to address regional economic underdevelopment by a federal government agency, which was abolished long before the work was finished. The project was located in Ottawa, at Statistics Canada. It employed several McGill graduate students, took more than ten years to complete, and was published in 1975 in four large volumes, two each in English and French. I suspect these publications were never consulted by more than a dozen people. In retrospect, it was a huge and costly waste of effort and energy, which frequently took me away from home, with regrettable costs to my family. Its most productive spinoff came in the form of collaboration with Lloyd Best in work on a multi-sectoral social accounting matrix designed for a stylized Caribbean "plantation economy." I recall that Tibor Barna, my former LSE teacher and practitioner of input-output techniques, advised me to abandon the work at Statistics Canada, which was no longer original, in favour of work on the plantation models. I regret that I lacked the imagination to follow his advice.

In 1963, McGill established the Centre for Developing Areas Studies (CDAS), and development economics became a subject area in the economics graduate program. In 1964, William Demas was invited as a Senior Visiting Research Fellow of CDAS, where he wrote *Economic Development of Small Countries, with Special Reference to the Caribbean* (1965). He returned to McGill University in 1967 to teach courses in the economics department on the history of economic thought and public finance. In 1965, the C.D. Howe Institute commissioned *Canada-West Indies Economic Relations* (1967), co-authored with Alister McIntyre. Work on the Best-Levitt Model of Plantation Economy started in a brainstorming session at St Augustine in 1964. In 1966, we obtained a modest two-year grant for a McGill-based project on "Externally Propelled Industrialization in the Caribbean." We produced four mimeographed volumes, the fourth containing studies on the bauxite industry by Norman Girvan and other associates of the project. In 1968, Lloyd Best presented "An Outline of a Model of a Pure Plantation Economy" to a West Indian conference on agricultural economics. For many years this was the only readily accessible publication of our work.

"ECONOMIC DEPENDENCE AND POLITICAL DISINTEGRATION: THE CASE OF CANADA"

In 1965, Charles Taylor invited me to draft background papers for the recently established New Democratic Party, on the controversial subject of foreign ownership, culminating in an oral presentation to the National Council of the NDP in May 1966. The text was elaborated in an essay published in the *New World Quarterly* in 1968 as "Economic Dependence and Political Disintegration: The Case of Canada." The first page of text quoted the Hon. Walter Gordon, President of the (Canadian) Privy Council, on the occasion of Canada Day, 1967: "The choice is clear. We can do the things which are necessary to regain control of our economy, and thus maintain our independence, or we can acquiesce in becoming a colonial dependency of the United States, with no future except the hope of eventual absorption." Prophetic words.

Revised and expanded with data on the corporate penetration of the world economy, grounded in economic analysis drawing on Schumpeter, Galbraith, Chandler, Mikesell, and Vernon, and marginally also on Polanyi, and documented by statistical data and testimony from leaders of U.S. multinational business, *Silent Surrender*: *The Multinational Corporation in Canada* (Macmillan of Canada, 1970) was a pioneering study of the effects of foreign direct investment on host countries. The book went through many printings and sold 40,000 copies. A French edition, with a postscript written after the October Crisis of 1970, was prefaced by Jacques Parizeau, then professor of public finance at the business school of the University of Montreal (HEC). *Silent Surrender* was widely reviewed, including an interview with me on the front page of the business section of the *New York Times*. A departmental committee on tenure and promotions, however, deemed it to be a "non-publication" for purposes of tenure. I return to *Silent Surrender* in commenting on the paper by Mel Watkins.

THE 1970S: BETWEEN TRINIDAD AND MONTREAL

In 1969 I obtained leave from McGill to take up a CIDA-financed appointment at the Institute of Social and Economic Research in Trinidad to continue my collaboration with Lloyd Best on plantation economy models. It was not to be. CIDA unexpectedly withdrew the promised support. Enquiries revealed intervention by Canadian security agencies, confirmed when a former student of mine employed by CIDA reported that he was shocked to see my file with a notation to kill this project on instruction of the RCMP. I then accepted an invitation from William Demas to go to Trinidad to direct the construction of multi-sectoral national economic accounts for Trinidad and Tobago, financed by a technical assistance program of the International Monetary Fund. The system was intended to serve as the data base for the next Four Year Plan, and would have integrated real and financial flows. I spent a full year in Trinidad, returning to Montreal in the autumn of 1970, to the October Crisis. For the next three years, I combined full-time teaching at McGill with long summers in Trinidad supervising the work.

When OPEC raised the price of oil in 1973, and new offshore deposits came along, all economic resource constraints were lifted. There was money to burn. Our work was abruptly terminated in 1973. Files and worksheets were locked up and my interim report was declared confidential. Long-term economic planning was abandoned. Senior technocrats were sent on indefinite leave. The University of the West Indies then offered me a three-year appointment as visiting professor at the Institute of International Relations, and I resumed work on the Best-Levitt Plantation Economy Models in 1974. Once again, political harassment intervened, when my work permit was inexplicably withdrawn in 1975 and I was ordered to leave the country. The university protested, but to no avail.

I have never been able to establish definitively on whose initiative this intervention was taken. What I do know is that Canadian security files almost cost me access to Statistics Canada in 1975 to complete my Atlantic provinces input-output studies, and that an invitation to join the governing board of the International Development Research Centre in 1978 failed to pass a security check. I was among many Canadians whose professional careers were adversely affected in the 1970s by the over-zealous activities of Canadian security agencies. This explains why I have never participated in official Canadian overseas development assignments.

The effect was to strengthen my determination to put my professional capacities at the service of Third World initiatives to redress the imbalance of power in the international economic system. In 1976 I worked on a study of the international bauxite aluminum industry for the United Nations Economic Commission for Latin America to assist host countries in bargaining with multinationals. Dudley Seers invited me to the Institute of Development Studies to continue the work on plantation economy, but I was too upset by all that had happened to take full advantage of my brief stay in Sussex. At the insistence of

George Beckford, the University of the West Indies offered a two-year appointment with the economics department on the Jamaica campus. I returned to Canada on the eve of the Jamaican election of 1980.

I put these facts on the record because I wish it to be known that links between Canada and the Caribbean relating to my work owe nothing to Canadian government agencies. They owe everything to bonds of friendship and mutual respect forged in intellectual and political struggles over many decades, evidenced in the generous tributes and kind words by Lloyd Best, Norman Girvan, Michael Witter, Mel Watkins, and Duncan Cameron.

THE 1980S: INSTITUTION BUILDING IN CANADA

The 1970s closed with the self-destruction of the Grenada Revolution and the American invasion of the island in 1983. This closed an era of Caribbean radicalism. These experiences, and the radicalization of the political climate in the 1970s, moved me toward a more institutional and historical approach to problems of development and underdevelopment. The 1980s were a period of consolidation of research and teaching – now exclusively in the area of economic development. Although I prepared a comprehensive background study for a Canadian parliamentary committee in 1982, developed a Caribbean Newsletter at McGill, and examined Haiti's national accounts for the World Bank in 1986, my concerns now shifted to a systematic review of post-war approaches to Third World development. This was motivated in part by concern that the rise of market fundamentalism was pushing development off the agenda of the international financial institutions. Crisis management displaced social, human, and even economic development. Development economics was disappearing from curricula of major North American universities. Fortunately the large number of Third World graduate students made it impossible to eliminate development as an area of specialization at McGill University. Under the auspices of the Development Committee of the Association of Universities and Colleges of Canada (AUCC), we surveyed teaching programs in international development studies at Canadian universities and produced a report, the "State of Development Studies in Canada" (1985). This was also the time I participated in initiatives to establish the Canadian Association for the Study of International Development (CASID) as a Learned Society. This and the establishment of the Karl Polanyi Institute of Political Economy at Concordia University in 1987 constituted my contribution to institution building in Canada.

1990S: BETWEEN JAMAICA AND MONTREAL

In 1989 I reduced McGill University teaching to half time, and in 1992 I retired from teaching at the university. For six years (1989–95) I taught a one-semester course, "Theories of Economic Development," in Jamaica at thc Consortium Graduate School of Social Science of the University of the West Indies, directed by Norman Girvan. It was the most enjoyable and rewarding experience in all my years of university teaching. The students were bright and highly motivated, and I could develop the material in an interdisciplinary direction without loss to the core of development economics. Teaching was accompanied by research on structural adjustment and Jamaica's external debt from 1970 to 1990, and other studies relating to Caribbean political economy. The most difficult and ultimately satisfying assignment was an Eric Williams Memorial Lecture at the Central Bank of Trinidad and Tobago on "Debt Adjustment and Development." From 1995 to 1997, I served as the first George Beckford Professor in Caribbean Political Economy. In the course of this two-year appointment, I edited *Caribbean Political Economy* (1996) jointly with Michael Witter, collected and introduced *The George Beckford Papers* (2000), and accepted all invitations which could take me to Trinidad.

Although I had visited many times since the early 1960s and spent two years there in 1978–80, it was not until the 1990s that I really got to know and to feel at home in Jamaica. In my Beckford lecture, "From Decolonization to Neoliberalism" (1995), I argued that the legacy of plantation slavery in the form of gross income disparities and a profound disrespect for the dignity of ordinary Jamaicans are at the root of Jamaica's stagnating economy, and that no amount of tinkering with macroeconomic variables can resolve this deep-rooted systemic crisis. I was told that income redistribution is not politically feasible. Be that as it may, Jamaica convinced me that we will have to reinvent socialism – in the traditional sense of social and economic equity.

Colleagues and friends who made my stays in Jamaica pleasant and productive are too numerous to mention, but very special thanks go to Michael Witter and Norman Girvan, whose constant support was critical in sustaining my belief in the importance of what I was doing. I don't know whether to thank or curse Norman for the seductive proposal that I pass on my "reading" of theories of economic development to future students in the form of a book. This project received constant encouragement from William Demas and financial support from the IDRC. Little progress has been made since 1997, but my debt to William

Demas alone makes it impossible to rest until I have completed this book. His last words to me were about its importance. I pray that I am granted the time and energy to repay this debt in the only currency that has validity. His insistence on the importance of recovering the insights of the great economists of the past has lost none of its urgency. Since the early 1980s, the international financial institutions have imposed financial and trade liberalization and privatizations on indebted developing countries. "Dependency" has disappeared from the development discourse, but the reality persists. Governments have been stripped of policy tools to defend societies from a predatory style of corporate capitalism. The imbalance of power in the world system is extreme, reflected in escalating inequalities in income, assets, and consumption of non-renewable resources, including the most basic necessities of life: soil, water, and clean air. In the flood tide of globalization, the small countries of the Caribbean are at risk of marginalization as playgrounds for tourists and sources of unwanted immigration.

CONTINUITY AND CHANGE IN THE CARIBBEAN

It is against this background that our attempts to theorize Caribbean economy on its own terms merit revisiting. Our models of plantation economies were developed in the late 1960s, to assist the transition to a more diversified and autonomous style of economic management. The methodology was historical and institutional, and traced plantation economy from its foundation in the mercantilist era, which preceded industrial capitalism (Model I), to its modification in the era of British free trade and emancipation of slave labour (Model II), and further modification in the age of the "mercantilism" of the modern multinational corporation (Model III). The models are abstractions, which capture continuity and change with emphasis on the relationship between "external" and "domestic" economic agents as "plantation economy" moves through these three phases. Although the models are constructed with economic actors, activities, and categories of income, they are powerful in explaining the legacy of the plantation on the social and political institutions of the Caribbean. Contemporary Caribbean economies bear the legacy of their origins as a slave plantations, established by metropolitan merchants and planters for the explicit purpose of producing an export commodity (sugar) for profit from sale on world markets. Our model of contemporary plantation economy has similarities with Samir Amin's "extraverted" peripheral capitalist economy, but it is both more specific and more detailed in the articulation of the mechanisms of the unequal incorporation of peripheral export economies in the international system. Specifically, plantation economies have inherited a local business class with planter behaviour and mentality, a peasantry and working class descended from slaves brought from Africa, and indentured labour from India.

When wage labour replaced chattel slavery on the plantations, a peasantry of former slaves developed a *residentiary peasant sector* of food production and small-scale craft manufactures for the domestic market along with some non-traditional agricultural export commodities. This trend toward an increasing supply of locally produced goods for domestic and export markets was reversed with the arrival toward the end of the nineteenth century of new corporate agribusiness and capital-intensive mining operations. The potential for self-reliant national development was frustrated, culminating in a system crisis in the 1930s. Post-war economic growth and development was driven by a (foreign-owned) export enclave sector and accompanied by import substitution of semi-luxury consumer goods by branch plants or licensed operations of metropolitan corporations. An active state sector provided infrastructure and tax concessions to foreign investors.

It was Lloyd's genius to perceive the manifold correspondence of the slave plantation with contemporary business practices of foreign – and also local – firms operating in the Caribbean environment. For Lloyd, the proprietors, merchants, planters, attorneys, and house and field slaves of the "Model of a Pure Plantation Economy" became a language to describe the metropolitan financial and merchant capitalists, the local margin-gathering merchants, the absentee foreign owners of multinational corporations, the resident local business classes with metropolitan consumption patterns and social aspirations, the managers of overstaffed private and public enterprises (complementing salaries with generous perks of housing, car, and travel allowances), and the working population – descendants of slaves and indentured labourers. The imagery has not lost its resonance, certainly not in Jamaica where a rising tide of popular anger at police brutality and the effective absence of justice for the poor and dispossessed recalls the Morant Bay Rebellion of 1865 and the labour riots of 1938.

Everybody who knows the history of the Caribbean – and that includes the Rastafarians, the Calypsonians, and others not schooled in the academy – knows that colonialism, imperialism, and capitalism came to this region with Columbus, 500 years ago. Lloyd Best has called it "The Enterprise of the Indies." The anniversary of 1492 was marked in three magnificent issues of the *Trinidad and Tobago Review*. Lloyd has sustained the vision of the Caribbean as a transnational cultural community, united by commonalities of history – the place where Africa with a creative dash of Asia was forced to practise

European institutions in the Americas. This is a vision of a unique Caribbean civilization. In these times of economic liberalization and diminishing political sovereignty, cultural commonalities can play an important role in the cohesions of regional blocs of developing countries. In the last years of his life, William Demas, architect of the Caribbean Community, mooted the idea of a political union of the Commonwealth Caribbean, starting with the micro countries of the OECS, and extending to embrace Trinidad, Barbados, and Guyana.

Much effort has gone into deepening and widening the Caribbean Community which now includes Haiti and Suriname together with the English-speaking countries of the Caribbean. Since the demise of Cuba's special relationship with Russia and East Europe, Cuba's economic links with her Caribbean neighbours have increased in importance. One of the institutions bridging linguistic and political barriers is the Association of Caribbean Economists (ACE), nurtured by Norman Girvan since its foundation in the mid-1980s. His deep commitment to Caribbean regionalism earned him the unanimous nomination by the governments of the Caribbean and Central America to the position of Secretary General of the Association of Caribbean States. The vision of the New World Movement lives on. Lloyd Best's "Independent Thought and Caribbean Freedom" has gained new significance in the era of a "globalization" which looks more like the extension of the American Empire to encompass the whole hemisphere. A generation of West Indians, influenced by the work of the so-called West Indian economists of the late 1960s and early 1970s, now occupy positions of importance as politicians and senior government advisors. They have made a significant contribution to the claims of small economies for special and differential treatment in international trade negotiations both in the World Trade Organization and the Free Trade Agreement of the Americas.

There have been many regrets that the Best-Levitt work on plantation economy has not been available in published form, to receive scholarly criticism and enable younger scholars to develop the work. As Lloyd Best stated more than once, the completion and publication of our common work was not his priority. For his purposes, the "Model of A Pure Plantation Economy" (1968) was sufficient to establish continuities of the legacy of the plantation on Caribbean economy and society and to underline commonalities of historical experience within the Caribbean. The failure to complete and publish the plantation economy models is one reason the work of Best, Beckford, Girvan, Levitt, and others failed to develop a "school" of Caribbean structuralist economics, with a core of younger scholars confident and able to challenge the resurgence of neo-classical economics. As Norman

Girvan observed, Lloyd Best has been constant in charting his own path, in his own way, with total determination to conduct unique and original theorizing. At all times on his own terms.

Our joint work of thirty years ago is now being prepared for publication. I believe that it remains a powerful explanatory device for understanding the persistence of the dysfunctional behaviour of the private and public decision makers in Caribbean society. The tensions and ambiguities in the work are an invitation to critical thought and creative innovation. Norman Girvan has provided a useful list of questions. How much explanatory power remains? Have diverging trajectories of development made it less relevant to treat Caribbean experience within the framework of one encompassing paradigm? What use is the model as a guide to policy? What are the key characteristics of the "residentiary" sector? Production for the domestic market? Local ownership of key industries? A native capitalist class? What role does race play? What does this imply for the role of the state? Is the informal sector the modern manifestation of the Caribbean "peasantry"? Are all informal activities to be regarded positively? What about crime and drug trafficking? Is regional economic integration possible in the context of general liberalization? These questions outline a useful start in a re-evaluation of the plantation economy paradigm. All I can say with certainty is that the legacy of plantation slavery has yet to be extinguished in the two Caribbean islands which contributed the most fabulous wealth to their respective metropoles in the past – Jamaica and Haiti. Nowhere in the Caribbean does the majority black population live in a state of poverty on the scale of Jamaica or Haiti. The reasons for that are deeply rooted in the history of these two important Caribbean island countries.

There remains the critical question of agents of change. The plantation models implicitly pointed to the small-scale independent "peasantry" as the force which could move Caribbean society forward toward self-directed paths of economic development. Beckford argued this most directly, but it is implicit also in the work of Best, who once wrote that his dream was a Caribbean-wide "sou sou," an indigenous form of savings which could wrest financial power from foreign banks. In the 1970s Beckford moved toward socialism, Marxism, black power, and Third World radicalism. Best maintained distance from all these tendencies, insisting that the Caribbean economy and society was a *sui generis* phenomenon, which could not be described in European terms of class. His aversion to socialism was manifest in his extreme hostility toward Michael Manley, but Fidel Castro was the only Caribbean politician who merited his respect. Lloyd is a complex man. As he said, his thinking and mine converged only at certain points. We came to our collaboration from different backgrounds, skills, political orientations, and vocations. I was – and remain – a socialist. Lloyd Best is essentially liberal in the philosophic sense of that term, with a deep suspicion of statism in any form. But none of our many disagreements can break the bond of respect and affection. He remains the most original and independent mind in the English-speaking Caribbean.

WHAT ABOUT CANADA?

Extended absences from Canada, concentration of my intellectual interests on economic and social issues of Third World development, and the evolution of Quebec toward an ever more "distinct" society have distanced me from Canadian political discourse. The world has shrunk, but the distance from Montreal to Toronto has increased. Mel Watkins is the exemplary model of the political economist he described so well as the "scholarly dissenter from orthodoxy and activist, or minimally providing nourishment for the political activist." But there is nothing minimal about Watkins, who has combined intellectual work with activism since I first knew him many years ago – and continues to do so within a (I hope) renewed New Democratic Party. He had the imagination to see how the Canadian "staple theory" could serve the struggle for Canadian economic sovereignty and independence. Mel Watkins is a Canadian left nationalist. Steady as a rock. He has never bent to fashion, whether the Marxism of the 1970s, or the postmodernism of the 1980s. "Nuff Respect," as they say in Jamaica!

I read with interest Mel's account of the new Canadian political economy and its influence in the institutionalization of Canadian Studies, within the larger domain of "cultural studies," where the emphasis on multiculturalism, difference, and identities reflects change and renewal in Canadian cultural and political life. Canada has become less "white" and somewhat less WASP. That is good. But what is left of Canadian nationalism? Indeed, what is left of the Canadian left? And dare I ask, what is left of Canada as a sovereign country? And who cares? Canada's economic élites are now firmly – even aggressively – continentalist. It was not always so but, on rereading *Silent Surrender*, I was reminded that eminent Canadian historians and philosophers thought that it was already too late thirty years ago to save "politics" from the continental drift of "economics." But "drift" is misleading, because every step along the way to the "recolonization" of Canada has been negotiated by the federal government, in exchange for favours and concessions granted to Canada by virtue of the "special relationship." The concessions were almost exclusively favours to Canadian exporters seeking secured market access in the United States. With every negotiation for "special treatment," Canada's national autonomy diminished, and vulnerability to U.S. pressures increased. In 1967, on the occasion of Canada's centennial, Prime Minister Pearson conceded that Canada was in no position to oppose the Vietnam war because "when you have 60 per cent or so of trade with one country, you are in a position of considerable economic dependence." So true, but Canada now has over 85 per cent of its trade with the United States. Mexico has bargained away its autonomy for a similar degree of trade dependence.

Canada's experience with the "special relationship" should serve as a warning to the rest of the Americas. The expansion of U.S. trade and investment by a "hub and spoke" strategy of bilaterally negotiated "special relationships" weaves an ever larger spider web of entrapment. In the 1960s, the price for market access, including the successful Canadian auto pact and exemption from an exchange equalization tax on bonds floated in the U.S. market, was the sacrifice of Canadian monetary autonomy. The story is worth recalling in light of the monumental fiasco of dollarization in Argentina. Forty years of opportunities to diversify the Canadian economy were lost. Canada emerged from the Second World War as a rising industrial power. In the 1960s, Canada was richer than Japan, and Korea was dirt poor. Today Korea has a successful indigenous automobile industry but Canada, with its branch-plant industry, is helpless as General Motors is closing its only plant in Quebec and Ford is closing plants in Ontario. Industrial workers of yesterday – and some of their children – are driving taxis, serving hamburgers at Macdonalds or working in low-wages call centres.

When *Silent Surrender* was written, we believed that Canada still had choices. I thought the book could help to strengthen the resolution of Canadians to regain effective control over the economy, as a precondition of a democratic social order. It gives me no joy that *Silent Surrender* was prophetic in its prediction of the political disintegration of Canada and its economic, and now also military, absorption into the American Empire. A century ago, it did not seem ridiculous to proclaim with Wilfrid Laurier, that "the twentieth century belongs to Canada," a pioneering young nation, looking to the future with great hope. Today, Canada as a sovereign country is history. In retrospect, we see that Canada led the industrial world in the relinquishing of national sovereignty. And the last nails in the coffin were struck as a direct consequence of September 11, 2001.

Within days of that event, the U.S. Ambassador informed Ottawa that Canada would have to relinquish sovereignty in refugee and immigration policy, and agree to the policing of a "common external perimeter." United States pressure was physical and irresistible. With 85 per cent of Canada's exports destined to U.S. markets, and container trucks backed up for miles, lengthy inspections of road transports at border crossings threatened to bring exports to a grinding halt. We will not know for some time how many other concessions Washington has extracted – or will extract – from Ottawa. But one thing is clear: Canada's treasured image as international peacekeeper has been thrown to the wolves of war. When Canada rejected the offer of a role in the United Nations-sponsored and European-led international peace keeping mission to Afghanistan to fight beside U.S. combat forces, under U.S. command, Lester Pearson might have wished to rise from the grave to return his Peace Prize.

I researched the issue of foreign ownership for a policy committee of the New Democratic Party in the early 1960s. The predominant view of economists influential within the social democratic left at that time was that foreign investment was beneficial to economic growth and any perceived threat to Canadian identity should be dealt with by explicit cultural policies. American capitalists were no worse and no better than Canadian capitalists and generally paid higher wages. Professor Harry Johnson, as unofficial dean of Canadian economists, was among my intellectual adversaries within the New Democratic Party. They argued the case for further and faster continental economic integration, and considered efforts to discourage takeovers or repatriate some foreign-owned sectors as misguided nationalism. The familiar economic argument was based on mainstream economic theory of comparative advantage of specialization. The response called for the deconstruction of the theory of the firm and the theory of international trade to take account of the implications of the arrival of the multinational corporation as the predominant economic enterprise.

My argument was that a subsidiary or branch plant of a multinational corporation is not an independent firm whose shareholders happen to be non-resident but an organic part of a production and marketing organization whose major decisions are taken with respect to the viability, security, expansion, and ultimately the global profitability of the enterprise as a whole. The last chapter of *Silent Surrender* documented the economic consequences of the control of Canada's leading industries by U.S. corporations. It drew on statistical and survey material, including the findings of the Watkins Report, and subsequent studies largely confirmed the results. The ultimate *political* consequences of the penetration of the Canadian economy by U.S. subsidiaries was treated in the concluding twelve pages of the last chapter, subtitled "Political Disintegration." I speculated that Quebec, whatever its constitutional status, might become a more viable and dynamic economy than the rest of Canada because its technocratic, professional, business, and political élite had a "more clearly defined sense of national purpose and a greater confidence in its ability to achieve its objectives." In a liberalized international economic environment, social cohesion and national purpose are critical assets in defense of "really existing" sovereignty.

THE NEW MERCANTILISM OF THE TRANSNATIONAL CORPORATION

The originality of *Silent Surrender*, which distinguished the work from other studies of the effect of foreign direct investment on host countries, was the historical perspective of Canada as a commodity exporting hinterland on, in Harold Innis's phrase, "the margin of western civilization." This owes intellectual debts to Innis, Canada's Scottish-born economic historian, to Latin American economic structuralist literature, and to my collaboration with Lloyd Best. The link between economic analysis and history is the concept of the "new mercantilism" of foreign direct investment. By this I did not mean trade protectionism but the modern transnational corporation (TNC) as a reincarnation of the Hudson Bay or East India Companies of the old mercantile capitalism. Like their forerunners, the large TNCs are private economic entities operating across borders and over distant oceans, with political support from the home base, and concessions extracted from host countries in unequal negotiations. These global corporations can switch sourcing and production locations, and they capture new markets by selling below costs of production. Transactions among parent, subsidiaries, and contract suppliers are at notional transfer prices, and financing is largely internal. Neither the parent nor the subsidiaries behave like the independent firm of textbook economics.

The "new mercantilism" illuminates structures of power underlying global markets. To a greater extent than is generally recognized, the structural features of pre-industrial mercantilism persist. They are instituted in political and economic "rules of the game," which bear the legacy of their origins in the formative pre-industrial era of the modern economic world order. The following five "rules of the game" are drawn on the work of Lloyd Best:

1 geo-political commercial spheres of influence;
2 peripheral exports of cheap labour whether embodied in agricultural, mineral products or low value-added manufactures;
3 metropolitan control over sources of finance, channels of distribution and communication, and access to technology;
4 "hard currency" as the only "real" money;
5 the "special relationship" between major metropoles and subordinate dependencies.

These insights form the link between the Best-Levitt plantation economy studies and my reading of Canada's slide into dependence and political disintegration. There are moreover, interesting similarities between the periodization appropriate to Canada and the English-speaking Caribbean, due to their common historic incorporation into Britain's Empire. In the Caribbean, British free trade and emancipation in the mid nineteenth-century opened opportunities for a "residentiary" sector serving domestic and external markets. In Canada, when British free trade loosened the ties of the old mercantile system, a creole class of (principally) Scottish Canadian entrepreneurs founded the Canadian state and designed a "national policy" which created an east-west economy geared to the exports of wheat to Britain and financed by British portfolio investment in railway and other infrastructure. When Canada's "special relationship" shifted from Britain to the United States, the national economy fractured into a set of north-south trade relations along 4,000 miles of common border. The "new mercantilism" of the U.S. subsidiaries and branch plants generated income growth, but resulted in the regression of Canada to a political and economic satelite.

If transnational corporate enterprise is a *micro economic* "throwback" to the pre-industrial era of merchant capital, the global dominance of financial over directly productive capital is its *macro economic* expression. The glories of early industrial capitalism were celebrated in iron and steel – the Eiffel Tower, the Crystal Palace, the grand railway stations and railway hotels. The icons of late twentieth-century capitalism are the financial and commercial towers of the major business centres of the world. Speculation in stock markets, currencies, and real estate, mergers, takeovers, and the enforced privatization of national assets are draining the economic life from viable economies, destroying employment, impoverishing the middle class, and creating a new underclass of the poor. This predatory model of capitalism invades all spaces: private and public, real and virtual, internally and externally. It is driven by greed and materialism gone mad. Economists are the high priests of this religion from Babylon, as the Rastafarians would say.

REINVENTING "SOCIALISM"?

As John le Carré famously remarked, the fact that communism has failed does not mean that capitalism will not also fail. In an important contribution to the symposium, Samir Amin maintains that the two great challenges now facing humanity – environmental disaster and global inequality on a scale unknown in all human history – call for a long and difficult transition from capitalism as we know it to nothing less than a civilizational transformation toward valuations of life and nature which depart radically from the "economic laws" of capitalism. He calls it "socialism." But whatever we may call it, it cannot be reduced to "capitalism without capitalists," whether evolutionary or revolutionary social democracy, Soviet-style communism, China's Maoism or any of the varieties of African socialism. Socialism has no meaning if it does not offer a civilization different from that produced by the capitalist cult of productionism, productivity, competitiveness, and "economism."

This new civilization will have to be built on the conservation of the limited resources of nature and a rejection of instrumental "productionist" approaches of capitalism (and all previous forms of socialism) which subordinate the needs of "society" to the needs of "the economy." This vision of socialism as a culture with a universalist vocation rejects appeals founded on ethnicity and religious diversity as well as reactionary cults of communitarianism. In that regard, globalization has positive aspects concerning the liberation of the individual and societies. Nor have historic efforts to transcend capitalism been unimportant. Western social democratic society is, as Asmin notes above, "the most advanced, attractive, and humane, even if viewed from the periphery, it has been associated with imperialistic attitudes."

Samir Amin definitively rejects the conventional Marxist ideas of capitalism and socialism as two separate systems. This dualistic concept suggests continuing conflict between the capitalist and the anti-capitalist forces within the framework of the "really exsting" capitalist world. In Amin's perspective, aspects of social democracy and market socialism form elements of a strategy by stages. The new civilization will develop within capitalism, the logic of capitalism co-existing with the (incompatible) logic of the requirements of social needs. The market must be made to assure social progress; various mixed forms of property – private, public, cooperative, informal, etc. – will continue to co-exist; the international system will have to be reformed to accommodate autonomous developmental policies and fundamental human rights, including social rights; and the acceptance of national and cultural pluralism, will have to be enforced by the rule of law.

There are evident similarities with Karl Polanyi's critique of capitalism, as noted on previous occasions, including the role of "anti-systemic movements" in Samir Amin's exposition, and Polanyi's "double movement." The concepts below, extracted from Samir's paper, underline his similarities with Karl Polanyi. Economic alienation is a phenomenon of full-scale industrial capitalism; the separation of political from economic life is a historical innovation, whereby "the economy appears to function by itself"; economic "laws" become objective forces; markets for commodities, labour, and capital appear to function "autonomously"; society is stripped of minimal control over the future because decision making is passed over to "automatic market forces," destroying the coherence of society.

It is important however, to remember that Polanyi's historical account of the tensions between the "economic" requirements of capitalism ("the market system") and the "social" requirements of society for protection from dislocation and instability was framed by the political jurisdiction of the nation-state. When historic conflicts could not be resolved within or between states, systemic breakdown occurred, as in the inter-war era. In the globalized economy of today, there are no economic or political "self-correcting" mechanisms to offset economic polarization or to redistribute the gains from economic growth on a global scale.

As Samir Amin noted, both mainstream and "anti-systemic" social thought have been "remarkably unconvincing" regarding accelerating global polarization. The influence on Marx and subsequent Marxist thought of the Enlightenment, with its powerful expressions of optimism and progress, whether social democratic or communist, suggested that capitalism would spread throughout the world – preparing the way for one integrated global society. This does not differ essentially from the "convergence" thesis of mainstream economics and World Bank advocacy of "globalization" on the grounds that "growth is good for the poor."

Traditional socialist thought and practice has also grossly underrated the environmental issue. The limitations of the planet's natural resources – and capacity to absorb industrial and urban waste – requires an economic calculus which is not based on short-term profitability or "efficiency" but which implies a different cultural and political civilization. "Here, in my view," says Samir, "we will have to break with a mode of thinking which accepts the prices that markets put on traded commodities and factors of production" as reflections of their true value in use. Equally if not more challenging is the development of a calculus of the essentials of personal and social well-being: security, affection, respect, participation, neighbourhood, friendship, family, festivals, etc.

In this brief recapitulation of Samir's paper, the ultimate challenge to capitalism is its inability to stem, even less to reverse, global polarization. Indeed the logic of unrestricted capitalism is to generate geographic divergence of income and wealth and social exclusion of the disadvantaged, as the essentials of daily life rise in price and subsistence economies shrink under pressure of external commercialization. Marx's pauperization, moderated and suppressed in the major capitalist countries, operates at the global level in a heterogeneous network of centres and peripheries.

In a lifetime of work, Samir Amin has made a pioneering contribution to our understanding of why polarization is inherent in the logic of capitalism, why poverty persists in "extraverted" peripheral economies, and why the reproduction of pre-capitalist (low productivity) modes of production is an integrated component of what Best and Levitt called the "overseas economy" of the metropoles. The story is briefly as follows: A pure form of capitalism cannot exist in reality, because it cannot grow and reproduce itself unless real wages rise with productivity. It would be threatened by permanent stagnation. In historical fact, events outside the logic of capitalism – revolutionary and imperialist wars, colonization, technological revolutions and anti-systemic class struggle which imposed higher remuneration for workers – have coincided with major phases of capitalist expansion. The historic compromise of the welfare state was such a period of strong capitalist expansion. Globalization is now eroding autocentric national production systems and weakening the power of labour.

Capitalist accumulation is currently in crisis. Seeking new markets and cheaper costs of production, capital expands into non-capitalist societies, generating polarizing globalization. But pre-capitalist low productivity modes of production persist in the domestic sectors of these societies. In peripheral economies open to free trade and the rule of the "law of one price," the population is impoverished. Resisted by the people who are its victims, it generates anti-systemic struggles against authoritarian and repressive regimes and popular strategies of survival which challenge the established capitalist order in many and various ways.

If capitalism could indeed renew itself to respond to the pressures of anti-systemic forces, can it not survive forever? Samir Amin does not think so, because there is no evidence that polarization has in the past diminished under these presures. On the contrary, it has accellerated them. Does this mean that capitalism will eventually be succeeded by a new consciousness, a new social (socialist) project? Not necessarily. Decadence is a very real possibility. Given the enormous power of destruction available to modern systems, humanity runs a high risk of self-destruction and collective suicide.

The risk is real, and advanced significantly in the opening years of the twenty-first century. The United States, with military capacity exceeding the combined forces of Russia, China, and Europe, is rolling back fifty years of progress in the construction of a civilized framework of international law. The objective of U.S. policy is not the dismantling of weapons of mass destruction, but the securing of an undisputed monopoly over their use. Political resistance to inequality and injustice, from whatever source or ideology, will be countered by military intervention against states, organizations, and individuals, wherever they may be. This is the meaning of the open-ended "war against terrorism." It is the military counterpart of a style of predatory financial capitalism which has more in common with the old mercantilism of piracy, conquest, and slavery than the very real achievements of an earlier phase of industrialization and economic development.

But this "new age colonialism" cannot establish the conditions of stability required for the reproduction of capital. The peoples of the world will assert their claim to freedom, dignity, and independence to shape their societies in their own way, for their own benefit. There will be civil wars as people confront corrupt regimes serving corrupt capitalists – foreign and domestic. The human spirit is indomitable. There is no way back to colonialism. The struggles will continue. Democracy, in its true meaning as "power to the people," has seized the imagination of the world.

NOTES

1 George Lamming, ed. *On the Canvas of the World* (Port of Spain: Trinidad and Tobago Institute of the West Indies, 1999). Foreword by Lloyd Best.

2 George Lamming, ed. *Enterprise of the Indies. Editor's Note.* (Port of Spain: Trinidad and Tobago Institute of the West Indies, 1999). Afterword by Lloyd Best.

3 They first met in Hamburg in 1970 at an extraordinary two-day workshop organized by Osvaldo Sunkel; the workshop brought together "dependency" theorists from several continents to meet and talk – and the talking went on late into the night.

Epilogue

DUNCAN CAMERON

What matters in academic life is the collegial pursuit of knowledge and understanding and the inspiration received from contact with others who share the quest. This book is homage to that tradition. Reflecting on these contributions, which include those of the scholars whose lives are honoured by this publication, we are struck by how ideas work themselves out to similar ends: they help us to discover communities of thought in dialogue and to see the world afresh.

Canadian intellectual life has been forever enriched by the presence among us of Gregory Baum and Kari Polanyi Levitt. That is the most obvious conclusion to be drawn from reading this volume. These distinguished thinkers have defined the field in which they work for many intellectuals, and no doubt for others still to come. The chapters show their ongoing influence in social ethics and theology where Gregory is a major figure, and political economy where Kari Levitt is so important.

The range of important and exciting questions addressed by some of the many people Gregory and Kari have inspired reflects the breadth and depth of each of their own interests and has made reading this book especially rewarding. For instance, in the first chapter, Ursula Franklin talked about planning and wanted to know about the effect on the people who were the object of the planning, the "plannees." Though a renowned metallurgist, she speaks with great familiarity of what social scientists have said about how those who are "being planned for" must be prepared to resist powerful forces in order to get on with meaningful lives. To arrive at her understanding of the place of technology in society requires not just crossing disciplinary boundaries several times, it means changing university faculties, moving from science to arts, to religious studies, and to social sciences.

Mel Watkins in his chapter shows how scholarship and politics are linked in Canadian political economy. Those who dared to develop a theory about Canada not "dependent" on imperial thinking have been able to help the rest of us make the voyage into Canadian consciousness. Original scholarship allows us to find out what the country is like, about the challenges it faces, and what it means to be a Canadian and a citizen in this world.

In her fine introduction Margie Mendell shows how the lives of Kari Polanyi Levitt and Gregory Baum have intertwined. Their intellectual interests are both so wide it would be surprising if they did not meet every so often. Gregory now studies the World Bank, which has been on Kari's list of favourite topics over the years. These pages also reveal – it could hardly be hidden – how different each of these two people is from the other in their scholarship, approach, and style of enquiry.

One of the attributes Kari and Gregory do have in common is what makes them so special. They both have first-class minds. Themes developed in their works speak to contemporary concerns and resonate with the intellectual heritage of the past. Both of these Montrealers are European by birth; their roots are deep in rich cultural soil of Germany, Austria and Hungary. Their lives in Canada reflect that European past, and each has contributed something to Canada that puts us in contact with the great intellectual currents of the wider world.

Gregory was a child in Berlin at a time when his Jewish ancestry put him at dire risk. His parents sent him to England. This prudence on their part undoubtedly saved him from Nazis death camps. Instead, the British interned him in Canada as an enemy alien. Alongside him were true Nazis and many refugees from Hitler. When, reluctantly, one asks about how horrible it must have been to have been encamped in Farnham, Quebec, Gregory talks about his experience as if it were a perpetual university seminar. "The best time of my life!" he exclaims. He was able to nourish his spirit under the most unenviable circumstances, and it is his spirit, not just his discipline and academic talent, that has carried him throughout his life.

Kari has roots in Budapest and Vienna through her own parents. True citizens of Red Vienna, neither Karl Polanyi nor Ilona Duczynska Polanyi would have had stood much of a chance at survival in Nazi-led Austria after the *anschluss*. Karl left for England in November 1933, and Kari was sent to join him in March 1934. Tempting fate, Ilona stayed on to participate in the illegal Schutzbund, rejoining her family in 1936.

Kari attended a pioneering boarding school in England, which had its own way of leaving a mark and its own cultural quirks, like the need to learn to wield a field-hockey stick. Her undergraduate university education was at the London School of Economics where the great debates over the future of society raged between students of Harold Laski and those of Hayek, with the socialist calculations controversies in which her father participated serving as a backdrop. At LSE Lionel Robbins was building a school that would also add another thinker from Vienna, the philosopher of science Karl Popper, a disgruntled socialist and anti-Marxist, to buttress its liberal economics.

Her appetite for a good argument and sharp debate, so much a part of her days in England, marks Kari's style to this day. The keen sense that well hidden behind the academic facade of much intellectual discourse is a real world of terrible problems is what distinguishes Kari Levitt. Her approach is to show how academic work conceals attitudes to the world that need to be revealed for all to know about. She sees, identifies, and explains what others are trying to pretend does not exist. She makes visible what the powers that be want to leave invisible. Much more money is being spent to buy intellectual work to cover up what is being done rather than to undertake independent research. While many intellectuals are busy serving power, Kari wants to get them out in the open for a real debate.

Reading this volume edited by Margie Mendell brings to mind the very nature of the Enlightenment project: the role of reason in society. The application of critical thought to what exists and what is possible supposes that society itself can be constituted in new ways, that it can somehow escape the many curses visited on the European civilization which gave birth to the Enlightenment. How often have we been reminded that the ideals which inspired modern European society could not stop the horror that overtook Europe: fascist terror, the extermination of six million Jews, Stalin's concentration camps and other sins committed in the name of communism?

What both Kari and Gregory represent in their own thought, and through the lives they have lived, is that these catastrophic events do not represent the failure of reason or of the Enlightenment project. Rather they underscore the need to develop the social, economic, and *intellectual* conditions under which enlightenment would be possible. Their work gets to the crux of the matter. Without a coherent world of thought in which science, social science, and works of the imagination and of the spirit lead to exchanges about how best to understand society, and how to see it changed, the enemies of enlightenment will continue to dominate the planet. The lessons to be learned from these two thinkers are about how to immerse yourself in a subject and how to make enquiry and intellectual exchange a way of life. Importantly, both these scholars have been uncommonly engaged with the world.

How shall we live in and beyond the latter part of the twentieth century, Kari Levitt has asked. Through a project "we the peoples of the United Nations" have named development, she has replied in articles, lectures, seminars, and exchanges with figures around the globe. Her work proceeded to analyze and describe development, casting light and critical comment on diverse works from W. Arthur Lewis to Dani Rodrik.

Kari has engaged with the most persistent of problems in the social sciences. The central theme in her work is to explain why some nations are rich and most people are poor. Her research has included an important contribution to our understanding of the Caribbean, as Lloyd Best, Norman Girvan, and Michael Witter have discussed in their chapters. Her ability to think for herself, and to see through what others would have us think, served in her good stead as she helped set out the plantation economy as a basic framework for understanding and thinking about the Caribbean experience. That work helps to explain many of the problems common to post-colonial societies, including Canada.

Her outlook suggests we should not be fooled by the spread of markets into thinking we have stepped out of history and found ourselves in a new era beyond power, money, state, and empire. In this, Kari is her father's daughter. We see Karl Polanyi in her when she shows us how to follow the historical development of the market economy to its sources. Here, she explains, you will find a hegemonic power, with its national money used internationally. Now, today, and for at least tomorrow, the U.S. is fulfilling the role Great Britain played in the nineteenth century, and the U.S. dollar has replaced the pound sterling as the key currency in the world. Bankers and investors are promoting trade and ownership of overseas assets; they are funding enterprises that are multinational in the scope of their activities. At the same time investment bankers are floating bonds and lending money to states for the military forces to maintain a regional and worldwide balance of power. But finance for state projects of a liberal character is part of the mix as well, so some money, not nearly enough, goes to develop education, means of cultural expression, and social and other government services.

Silent Surrender is well known as a penetrating analysis of the impact of foreign ownership on Canada, an account of the conditions under which Canada has put its very political existence as a sovereign state at risk. The book was reissued in 2002, over thirty years after its first publication. It has staying power because it also contains one of the best critiques of neo-classical economics ever published. And in that work

Kari sets out her thesis about the U.S. and the world economy, one of the first, and best, accounts of what is now known as globalization.

Kari shows us how to watch the working out of hegemony through the expansion of dollar investment throughout the world. She measured it for the period 1900 to 1966. In every economic sector, and in every part of the world, in all years except a few during the Depression, the amount of new money flowing into the U.S. was greater than the flow of U.S. investment abroad. Foreign ownership profits the foreign owner first and foremost. Next, she pointed to the buildup abroad of balances of U.S. dollars, not just in central bank reserves, but in the hands of private agents for local trade and investment and especially in what have become the vast Euro markets for finance, insurance, and commercial lending.

The rest of the world is lending to the U.S., explained Kari, while the U.S. is buying up their assets and funding military expansion, including the incredible nuclear arms race, which continues despite the withdrawal of its main adversary, the former Soviet Union, from the competition. That is the way the U.S. dominates the world. And, as Kari writes in her chapter in this volume, the U.S. does not seek the elimination of the weapons of mass destruction, it wants an undisputed monopoly over weapons of mass destruction.

A better world would take on the challenge of nuclear non-proliferation: those countries without nuclear weapons agree not to develop them, in return the nuclear powers agree to phase them out. This would be the logical solution, the application of reason to human affairs, the enlightened approach. The U.S. has for now abandoned that avenue. One is reminded of the story about Governor Adlai Stevenson, two-time Democratic candidate for the U.S. presidency against Eisenhower. After a stirring speech, an exuberant supporter came up to congratulate him and urge him on, "Mr Stevenson you are going to get the vote of every thinking American." "Thank you, Madam," he replied, "that won't be enough ... it takes a majority."

Pope John XXIII called development the new word for peace in a speech made in Yankee Stadium in New York. Nothing less than the temple of baseball would do for his American visit it seemed. That was back in the period known, with not a little affection, as the sixties, the first decade to be named by the United Nations a development decade. At that time in his life Gregory Baum was an advisor to Vatican II, the great transformation proposed for the Roman Catholic Church. He was also a Catholic priest and a professor of theology at St Michael's College, University of Toronto. With Northrup Frye, Marshall McLuhan, and C.B. Macpherson, he was one of the internationally renowned figures in that university.

When Gregory gave the Massey Lectures, the prestigious annual series broadcast by the CBC and published under the title *Compassion and Solidarity*, he addressed some of the questions that had been central to his life work, especially the issues that arise from Catholic social thought. These include the priority of the needs of labour over the wants of capital, the preferential option for the poor, and the need for the Church to embrace liberation theology. These are some of the same themes that defined many of his readers' understanding of what it means to be a Catholic in today's world.

For those of his many friends involved in social action in the community, Gregory is an ally, a fellow activist, and a generous contributor of time and money to each collective effort. But Gregory's action is not just political and it is about more than the community cause. Through participating with others in common work he is living his Catholic faith, fulfilling his religious beliefs in his daily life. Much of religious life is about adding hope to life, as Denis Goulet discusses in his chapter.

While he has a worldwide reputation in the Catholic faith community as a theologian teaching and reflecting upon his own faith, not even the Catholic Church is big enough to contain Gregory. He has written and taught about Protestant thought and theology in Canada and in the former German Democratic Republic. One of Gregory's many regular activities is as editor of *The Ecumenist*, reflecting the extension of his interest into every form of religious expression. In Western society theology and philosophy separated into distinct pursuits, but this is not the case in other societies. The contribution by Arvind Sharma shows us what happens when the "rights talk" of the West meets the concern for human dignity of the East.

At the age of sixty-three, Gregory was invited to continue to add to his career achievements by moving to McGill. He and Shirley were eager to return to live in Quebec, where he has formed close relationships over the years. As readers of Carolyn Sharpe's chapter will have discovered, Gregory Baum has established a special relationship with Quebec, where he has been warmly welcomed and well appreciated. Not only did Gregory explore and write about nationalism in Quebec and compare it to other great nationalisms in the world, he also wrote about the Catholic Church in Quebec and what it has meant to collective life.

One home for Gregory is the francophone journal *Rélations*. Another has been the Polanyi Institute, where his work intersects with that of Kari Polanyi Levitt. Gregory decided to write about Karl Polanyi and worked in the archives of the Institute to produce his significant exploration, *Karl Polanyi on Ethics and Economics*. Both Gregory and Kari participate actively in the daily political and social life of Quebec, and of Montreal. An important connection is their friendship with Polanyi Institute Director Margie Mendell. And their work, however different, does exhibit some interesting parallels. Both can write and speak about the most profound issues facing humanity in common language, accessible to all literate people, and not just other specialists. Indeed for those who hold that clarity of thought ranks at or near the top of intellectual qualities, both Kari and Gregory are especially prized.

Kari and Gregory are the same age and have lived through the same fervent debates and general turmoil of world affairs. It is fair to say that both of them are part of what has been called a democracy movement and (though it is harder perhaps to understand today) what was once proudly known as a socialist movement. This was, of course, before the usage and sense of the word became devalued by opponents and, even more hideously, by many of its own proponents. The contribution by Samir Amin recreates for readers of any age the atmosphere of the great socialist debates of the past century, and gives us convincing reasons to believe that differences among capitalists and among anti-capitalists should ensure much heated debate to come. His account of the world economy in crisis is sobering; but he has opened new perspectives on our times and suggested new ways of thinking about issues that matter to people. How shall we govern ourselves? And can we live an authentic life in harmony with nature and each other?

"I am responsible for my own life and I will make my own way in the world." Liberals and socialists able to agree with such a statement; both value individual freedom. But for socialists, that we come into the world as foundlings, totally dependent on others for support and sustenance until we are into our teenage years, means our very identities are forged by our relationships with others, and we cannot be ourselves without them. In order to exercise freely our latent capacities and capabilities, we require the presence and support of others. So we are primarily social beings.

This sort of "generic" socialism mobilized many people to search for a better way of life for all. Its spirit lives on in the democratic movement world wide, a movement for human liberation. It is pointless to argue over words such as socialism, it is after all the meaning that matters not the label. Perhaps what we have mostly in these pages is humanism. In the words of Edward Said in *The Guardian* (2 August 2003): "Humanism is the only, and I would go as far as to say the final resistance we have against the inhuman practices and injustices that disfigure human history."

It is appropriate to conclude on a celebratory note. For all their highly developed critical capacities, both Kari and Gregory have positive outlooks on the world. Neither is a stranger to sadness, but each lives very much in the present, looks forward to the next moment, and anticipates good times to come with friends or family.

When I first met Kari we were part of a group standing in a circle at a friend's cottage in the Gatineau Hills. "What was it like in Jamaica?" she was asked. Her eyes began to gleam, the sentences began to flow, and before long she had me seeing the people taking off the crops, loading the boats, and walking the streets. I could hear the music of the islands, the picture she painted of the society was that vivid. The sheer joy of being within hearing distance of Kari when she has a story to tell or something to say is something no one who knows her can forget.

When Gregory and I first met it was to talk about what became a joint book, *Ethics and Economics: Canada's Catholic Bishops on the Economic Crisis*. We had lunch at a small cafe near the University of Ottawa, the first of the regular meetings and meals together I so look forward to. His enjoyment of life is infectious. He loves to go to parties, laugh with friends, and meet new people. His enthusiasm for each of his projects never diminishes.

There are so many good words that somehow we do not see used together often enough. Friendship, wit, happiness, laughter, warmth, understanding, hope, honesty, fulfillment, they speak to our experience in the company of Gregory and of Kari. Thanks to Margie Mendell and the contributors, we are able to add to our knowledge of these two remarkable individuals. Thanks to this work, further evidence of the contributions of Kari Polanyi Levitt and Gregory Baum to scholarly life is available for future generations.

Selected Publications

GREGORY BAUM

That they May Be One. Westminster, MD: Newman Press, 1958.

The Jews and the Gospel. Westminster, MD: Newman Press, 1961; revised edition paperback under the title, *Is the New Testament Antisemitic?*

Progress and Perspective. Kansas City, MO: Sheed and Ward, 1962; paperback edition under the title, *Catholic Quest for Christian Unity*. New York: Paulist Press, 1965.

Ecumenical Theology Today. New York: Paulist Press, 1965.

The Credibility of the Church Today. New York: Herder & Herder, 1968.

Faith and Doctrine. Westminster, MD: Newman Press, 1969.

Man Becoming. New York: Herder & Herder, 1970.

New Horizon. New York: Paulist Press, 1972.

Religion and Alienation. New York: Paulist Press, 1975.

Truth Beyond Relativity: Karl Mannheim's Sociology of Knowledge. Marquette Lecture. Milwaukee, WI: Marquette University Press, 1977.

The Social Imperative. New York: Paulist Press, 1979.

Catholics and Canadian Socialism. New York and Toronto: Paulist Press, Lorimer, 1980.

The Priority of Labour: Commentary on John Paul II's "Laborem exercens." New York: Paulist Press, 1982.

Ethics and Economics (with Duncan Cameron). Toronto: Lorimer, 1984.

Theology and Society. New York: Paulist Press, 1986.

Solidarity and Compassion. New York and Toronto: Paulist Press, Anansi Press, 1988.

The Church in Quebec. Ottawa: Novalis, 1992.

Essays in Critical Theology. Kansas City, MO: Sheed and Ward, 1994.

Karl Polanyi on Ethics and Economics. Montreal: McGill-Queen's University Press, 1996.

The Church for Others: Protestant Theology in Communist East Germany. Grand Rapids, MI: Eerdsman, 1996.

Nationalism, Religion and Ethics. Montreal: McGill-Queen's University Press, 2001.

Frieden für Israel: Israeli Peace-and-Human Rights Groups in Israel. Paderborn: Bonifatius Verlag, 2002.

KARI POLANYI LEVITT

Kari Polanyi Levitt, ed. *The Life and Work of Karl Polanyi.* Montreal: Black Rose Books, 1990.

Kari Polanyi Levitt, and Michael Witter, eds. *The Critical Tradition of Caribbean Political Economy.* Kingston, Jamaica: Ian Randle Publishers, 1996.

Kari Polanyi Levitt and Kenneth McRobbie, eds. *Karl Polanyi in Vienna.* Montreal: Black Rose Books, 2000.

The George Beckford Papers. Selected and Introduced by Kari Levitt. Jamaica: University of the West Indies Press, 2000.

The Right to Development, Fifth Sir Arthur Lewis Memorial Lecture. Eastern Caribbean Central Bank. St Kitts, West Indies: Bassterre, 2000.

Silent Surrender, the Multinational Corporation in Canada. Toronto: Macmillan of Canada, 1970; re-issued with a new introduction, Carleton Library Series. Montreal: McGill-Queen's Press, 2003.

Reclaiming Development: A Caribbean Perspective on Globalization. Kingston, Jamaica: Ian Randle Publishers. Forthcoming.

Kari Polanyi Levitt and Lloyd Best. *Plantation Economy: A Historical and Institutional Approach to Caribbean Economic Development.* Forthcoming.